THE PRAYERS
OF PETER MARSHALL

Peter Marshall was born in Scotland. In
1927, aged twenty-five, he emigrated to the
United States, and before long began working towards his ministerial career. Within
nineteen years he had risen to Chaplain of
the United States Senate. His sincerity,
together with his gifts as a public speaker,
had already made his name famous through
the Southern States; but it was in the great
New York Avenue Presbyterian Church in
Washington that he reached the height of
his power. He died at the age of
forty-six in 1949.

The Prayers of
PETER MARSHALL

Edited and with
Prefaces by
CATHERINE MARSHALL

Collins
FOUNT PAPERBACKS

First published in Great Britain by Peter Davies, 1955
First issued in Fontana Books 1966
Reprinted in Fount Paperbacks January 1977
Tenth impression December 1985

© 1955 by Catherine Marshall

Made and printed in Great Britain by
William Collins Sons & Co. Ltd, Glasgow

TO THE PEOPLE OF PETER'S THREE CONGRE-
GATIONS, COVINGTON, ATLANTA, WASH-
INGTON, WHO WERE HIS INSPIRATION IN
THE MINISTRY OF PRAYER, THIS BOOK IS
AFFECTIONATELY DEDICATED

CONTENTS

Prayers for the Nation and the World

THE SENATE PRAYERS

ON THE THRESHOLD OF TIME

Early in the year 1947 many Americans began to realise that a man with an extraordinary talent for prayer had been made Chaplain of the United States Senate. Immediately, Peter Marshall's Senate prayers began to receive a great deal of national publicity.

Thus the nation at large suddenly "discovered" and grew enthusiastic about what Dr. Marshall's congregations had long known. For these congregations in Covington and Atlanta, Georgia, and in the Nation's capital, their minister's pastoral prayers had always been a unique experience in worship.

In the process of editing the prayers for this book, it has been easy to recapture my first fresh impression of the prayers as I, then a college student, originally heard them in Atlanta's Westminster Presbyterian Church in the winter of 1932.

It was immediately apparent to me that the morning prayer was for this young minister not just another customary, trite part of his order of service. The prayer period was approached in a leisurely fashion with an unmistakable sincerity and an undercurrent of anticipation approximating excitement.

"The most precious moments of our morning worship are the moments we spend with the Risen Lord," Peter would say before he began to pray. "We cannot see His form, but we can feel His presence. He knows all about you—your hidden perplexity, your secret shame. He waits by appointment, anxious to speak to you reassuringly, comfortingly, forgivingly. You may tell Him your needs now in your own way." Then a period of silence would follow.

Peter *knew* Christ was there, and he was somehow able to transmit that knowledge to the waiting congregation bowed before him. That was why hungry-hearted people would make almost any sacrifice to get to Westminster Church.

It was also obvious that Peter Marshall confidently expected things to happen as he prayed. Burdened consciences were going to be forgiven; burdened minds were going to be unloaded of worry and tension. The sick were going to be healed. The lonely were going to find a Friend. The aged were going to receive the benediction of a strange new peace.

It was this expectation of answered prayer that accounted for the undercurrent of excitement. And it worked! It was because many individuals in those congregations actually did have experiences of specific needs met that people came to regard these prayers as rare spiritual treasure.

There were other initial impressions—the young minister always clasped his big labouring-man's hands around the pulpit microphone in a characteristic gesture; his eyes were closed; he used no written prayer or even notes. The prayers flowed from the depths of his soul clothed in a rare beauty of language; yet there was the paradox of a simple dignity combined with a homey, down-to-earthness. . . . "Our heads swell so much easier than our hearts," he might say. Humour often crept in. . . . "We thank Thee, Lord, that there is no weather in heaven."

Those were my first impressions. At the end of Peter's ministry as at the beginning, all of this was still characteristic of him. Yet as the years went on, his prayers revealed a deepening of the channel of Peter's own Christian experience.

In Atlanta his prayers had been largely directed to the individual's needs. He spent little more time than does the average minister on petitions concerning the Nation or its leaders.

In Washington this changed. It was as if Peter saw all of life as from the perspective of a mountaintop. Three tributaries of interest, easily traceable in his later prayers, were the result.

First, he came to have a profound concern for his adopted country—more than a concern, a passion reminiscent of that of the seers and the prophets of ancient Israel. There was born in Peter's heart an ineffable yearning over America. He longed to see us " cast off all Pharisaical garments, lay down the overcoats of our smug complacence "; put aside self-interest and false pride, and become truly righteous, so that the United States of America might rise to her God-appointed destiny of world leadership.

There is little wonder that Dr Marshall was called to serve on Capitol Hill. Without realising it, he had been preparing for that task for years. The proof is that well over half of the total wordage of his pastoral prayers left to us are the outpouring of his heart on this patriotic note.

Peter's second great concern was for plain homespun virtues of honesty, integrity, and goodness of the individual. This was a natural corollary of his eagerness for righteousness on a national scale. He saw clearly that we can never achieve nationally what we are unwilling to accede to individually. Over and over he kept calling us back to these basic realities because he well knew that God is more impressed by an honest income-tax return than by any amount of too-stereotyped churchgoing.

The third strand of Peter's concern was that we be " more kindly affectioned, one to another, more patient, more understanding, forgiving one another even as God for Christ's sake has forgiven us." As searing tongues of misunderstanding and hatred leaped out to engulf the earth in World War II, this emphasis became an ever-recurring note in Peter's praying.

Because Peter did not write his prayers out, most of them are now lost to us. Were it not for the interest and ingenuity of three individuals, this collection of his pastoral prayers would not have been possible. In Atlanta, Peter Marshall's secretary, Ruby Coleman Daughtry, once took down a few of his prayers in shorthand. In Washington there was a girl in the State Department to whom Dr Marshall's prayers were soul sustenance. She conceived the idea of taking them down in shorthand during the church service. It proved to be hard dictation to get. A few words were irretrievably lost here and there. Nevertheless, the result was a group of prayers from which most of those included here are taken.

Of Miss Elizabeth McNaull's notes on these prayers, eighteen of them Dr Marshall subsequently corrected and edited himself, and included with his sermons which were then being printed locally in pamphlet form.

The only other pastoral prayers left to us are a residue of thirteen prayers recorded on tape along with the Sunday morning sermons. This was a labour of love undertaken by Mr Jack Ingram of Dallas, Texas, during the winter of 1947-1948, while he was stationed in Washington. Otherwise, I have only fragments of prayers jotted down by unidentified individuals.

The pastoral prayers were, of course, quite long. In

order to make them more readily usable by families and for individual devotions, I have taken the liberty of dividing them topically into prayers for various needs and occasions.

Dr Marshall had a way of speaking to the deepest needs of our hearts, because he actually was pouring out before the Throne of Grace the deepest needs of his own heart. In these particularly personal portions of the prayers I have changed the " we " of the public prayer to the even more personal " I." Otherwise the language is entirely Peter Marshall's.

In the prayer of Sunday morning, 26th December, 1948, there are these words: " We all need Thee so much. Grant that in the new year, if we shall live through it. . . ."

Did Peter Marshall have some intimation that the adventure men call dying was for him only thirty days away? I cannot be sure.

Perhaps it was just that he had so often seen death rudely interrupt men and women in the thick of life. Perhaps it was that he himself had long since quietly accepted the idea (since his first heart attack) that death stood always just at his elbow.

Whatever the reason, toward the end of the prayer there crept in an almost incredible sentence . . . " We are standing," Peter prayed, " on the threshold of time."

We are indeed—every one of us. That is why these prayers, breathed from the depths of a man's soul speak with surety to your heart and mine.

Catherine Marshall

Washington, 20th May, 1954

OUR SEEKING GOD

Our Father, sometimes Thou dost seem so far away, as if Thou art a God in hiding, as if Thou art determined to elude all who seek Thee.

Yet we know that Thou art far more willing to be found than we are to seek. Thou hast promised " If with all Thy heart ye truly seek me, ye shall ever surely find me." And hast Thou not assured us that Thou art with us always?

Help us now to be as aware of Thy nearness as we are of the material things of every day. Help us to recognise Thy voice with · much assurance as we recognise the sounds of the world around us.

We would find Thee now in the privacy of our hearts, in the quiet of this moment. We would know, our Father, that Thou art near us and beside us ; that Thou dost love us and art interested in all that we do, art concerned about all our affairs.

May we become aware of Thy companionship, of Him who walks beside us.

At times when we feel forsaken, may we know the presence of the Holy Spirit who brings comfort to all human hearts when we are willing to surrender ourselves.

May we be convinced that even before we reach up to Thee, Thou art reaching down to us. These blessings, together with the unexpressed longing in our hearts, we ask in the strong name of Jesus Christ, Our Lord. Amen.

THE HUMANITY OF JESUS

May our prayer, O Christ, awaken all Thy human reminiscences, that we may feel in our hearts the sympathising Jesus.

> Thou hast walked this earthly vale and hast not forgotten what it is to be tired, what it is to know aching muscles, as Thou didst work long hours at the carpenter's bench.
> Thou hast not forgotten what it is to feel the sharp stabs of pain, or hunger, or thirst.

Thou knowest what it is to be forgotten, to be lonely. Thou dost remember the feel of hot and scalding tears running down Thy cheeks.

O we thank Thee that Thou wert willing to come to earth and share with us the weaknesses of the flesh, for now we know that Thou dost understand all that we are ever called upon to bear.

We know that Thou, our God, art still able to do more than we ask or expect. So bless us, each one, not according to our deserving, but according to the riches in glory of Christ Jesus, our Lord. Amen.

I NEED THEE, LORD

I do need Thee. Lord, I need Thee now. I know that I can do without many of the things that once I thought were necessities, but without Thee I cannot live, and dare not die.

I needed Thee when sorrow came, when shadows were thrown across the threshold of my life, and Thou didst not fail me then. I needed Thee when sickness laid a clammy hand upon my family, and I cried to Thee, and Thou didst hear. I needed Thee when perplexity brought me to a parting of the ways, and I knew not how to turn. Thou didst indicate the better way. And though the sun is shining around me today, I know that I need Thee even in the sunshine, and shall still need Thee tomorrow.

I give Thee my gratitude for that constant sense of need that keeps me close to Thy side. Help me to keep my hand in Thine and my ears open to the wisdom of Thy voice.

Speak to me, that I may hear Thee giving me courage for hard times and strength for difficult places; giving me determination for challenging tasks. I ask of Thee no easy way, but just Thy grace that is sufficient for every need, so that no matter how hard the way, how challenging the hour, how dark the sky, I may be enabled to overcome.

In Thy strength, who hast overcome the world, I make this prayer. Amen.

" And it shall come to pass, that before they call,
I will answer ; and while they are yet speaking, I
will hear." *Isaiah* 65 : 24

Once again, our Father, we marvel at the mystery of Thy love
that can regard our low estate and can be concerned with
our weakness and our need, when Thou hast so many children
all around the earth with so much need and sin and sorrow.

Yet, in Thy great Love, Thou dost stoop to listen to us.
May the wonder of it enthrall our hearts, and the meaning
of it captivate our wills.

Make strong our faith that Thou art listening to us even
now, that the petitions rising from our hearts are heard by
Thee and have set in motion all the processes of divine
love, and caused to hurry to our assistance the spiritual
messengers at Thy command.

*In this faith, will you now tell your own needs to Him
who waits for you, by appointment, waiting to speak to you
reassuringly, comfortingly, forgivingly? Let us speak to Him
and hear Him speak to us. . . .*

TEACH US TO PRAY

Lord, teach us to pray. Some of us are not skilled in the
art of prayer. As we draw near to Thee in thought, our
spirits long for Thy Spirit, and reach out for Thee, longing
to feel Thee near. We know not how to express the deepest
emotions that lie hidden in our hearts.

In these moments, we have no polished phrases with
which to impress one another, no finely moulded, delicately
turned clauses to present to Thee. Nor would we be confined to conventional petitions and repeat our prayers like
the unwinding of a much-exposed film. We know, our
Father, that we are praying most when we are saying least.
We know that we are closest to Thee when we have left
behind the things that have held us captive so long.

We would not be ignorant in prayer and, like children,
make want lists for Thee. Rather, we pray that Thou wilt
give unto us only what we really need. We would not make
our prayers the importuning of Thee, an omnipotent God,

to do what we want Thee to do. Rather, give us the vision, the courage, that shall enlarge our horizons and stretch our faith to the adventure of seeking Thy loving will for our lives.

We thank Thee that Thou art hearing us even now. We thank Thee for the grace of prayer. We thank Thee for Thyself. Amen.

THE SOUL TONIC OF PRAYER

Father, I am beginning to know how much I miss when I fail to talk to Thee in prayer, and through prayer to receive into my life the strength and the guidance which only Thou canst give. Forgive me for the pride and the presumption that make me continue to struggle to manage my own affairs to the exhaustion of my body, the weariness of my mind, the trial of my faith.

In a moment like this I know that Thou couldst have worked Thy good in me with so little strain, with so little effort. And then to Thee would have been given the praise and the glory. When I neglect to pray, mine is the loss. Forgive me, Lord.

Let not, I pray, any future forgetfulness of mine, or a false sense of self-sufficiency, any spiritual laziness, or doubt of Thy faithfulness keep me from taking everything to Thee in prayer.

And now, I thank Thee that the fresh breath of heaven is even now blowing away the close, damp air of all my failure, of every doubt and fear. I ask Thee for that soul tonic of prayer that shall reburnish my faith, brighten my hope, revive and rekindle my love. In Thy name, I pray. Amen.

THE PROMISES OF GOD

O Lord Jesus, I remember that Thou hast said, "Lay not up for yourselves treasures upon earth, where moth and rust doth corrupt. . . ." O God, deliver me from falling in love with things. Help me rather to love people, to love principles, to love righteousness, to love Thee.

Thou hast commanded me " to seek first the Kingdom of

God and His righteousness," and then hast made me a promise that if my heart and mind and soul and will were thus dedicated, I should receive as dividends the very things I seek—an abundant ministry unto all my needs.

O God, help me to believe this. Help me to practise it, that I may find for myself that the promise is true, that all my needs shall be met.

Thou hast invited me "to ask, to seek, to knock "—assuring me that if I ask, it shall be given unto me; if I seek, I shall find; if I knock, it shall be opened unto me.

Help me to believe that, O God. Give me the faith to ask, knowing that I shall receive. Give me the faith to seek, believing that I shall surely find. Give me the faith and the persistence to knock, knowing that it shall be indeed opened unto me.

Help me to live the Christian life in daring faith and humble trust, that there may be worked out in me, even in me, Thy righteousness and goodness. With a sense of adventure, I make this prayer. Amen.

FOR MORE FAITH

Forgive us, O God, for our small concept of the heart of the Eternal, for the doubting suspicion with which we regard the heart of God.

Give to us more faith. We have so little . . . we say. Yet we have faith in each other—in cheques and banks, in trains and aeroplanes, in cooks, and in strangers who drive us in cabs. Forgive us for our stupidity, that we have faith in people whom we do not know, and are so reluctant to have faith in Thee who knowest us altogether.

We are always striving to find a complicated way through life when Thou hast a plan, and we refuse to walk in it. So many of our troubles we bring on ourselves. How silly we are . . .

Wilt thou give to us that faith that we can deposit in the bank of Thy love, so that we may receive the dividends and interest that Thou art so willing to give us. We ask it all in the lovely name of Jesus Christ our Saviour. Amen.

CONFESSION

O Lord, I come to Thee out of my great need. Thou hast pledged Thy word that whosoever cometh to Thee shall in no wise be cast out.

I dare to pray that something will happen to me in Thy presence. Lord, I know I need to be changed! For the visions that once swept across the leaden skies of monotony, like white-winged gulls, have dimmed and faded, and I would see them again. Open Thou my eyes!

Shame fills my heart as I remember the aspirations that I have breathed before Thee, the vows I made, the resolves that were born, the seedlings of consecration that were planted in my heart. I blush to remember the withering blight that touched them all—my failures, my shortcomings.

Lord, I confess before Thee that:

I have had longings and nudges from Thee which I did not translate into action.

I have made decisions without consulting Thee, then have blamed Thee when things went wrong.

I have said that I trusted Thee, yet have not turned my affairs over to Thee.

I have been greedy for present delights and pleasures, unwilling to wait for those joys which time and discipline alone can give.

I have often sought the easy way, have consistently drawn back from the road that is hard.

I have been fond of giving myself to dreams of what I am going to do sometime, yet have been so slow in getting started to do them.

Forgive me for all the intentions that were born and somehow never lived. These, Lord Jesus, are sins, grievous in Thy sight, grievous even in mine.

And now I claim Thy promise to change me. Do Thou for me what I cannot do for myself. Lead me into a new tomorrow with a new spirit. Cleanse my heart, create within me new attitudes and new ideas, as only Thou canst create them.

For these good gifts, I thank Thee, Lord. Amen.

WITH SORROW AND TRUE
REPENTANCE

Forgive me, Lord Jesus, for the things I have done that make me feel uncomfortable in Thy presence. All the front that I polish so carefully for men to see, does not deceive Thee.

For Thou knowest every thought that has left its shadow on my memory. Thou hast marked every motive that curdled something sweet within me.

I acknowledge, with sorrow and true repentance, that
I have desired that which I should not have;
I have toyed with what I knew was not for me;
I have been preoccupied with self-interest;
I have invited unclean thoughts into my mind and entertained them as honoured guests;
My ears have often been deaf to Thy whisper;
My eyes have been often blind to the signs of Thy guidance.
Make me willing to be changed, even though it requires surgery of the soul, and the therapy of discipline.

Make my heart warm and soft, that I may receive and accept now the blessing of Thy forgiveness, the benediction of Thy " Depart in peace . . . and sin no more." In Jesus' name. Amen.

CLEANSE ME, O GOD

" If we confess our sins, he is faithful and just to forgive us our sins, and to cleanse us from all unrighteousness." *I John* 1 : 9

Father, over and over again I have fallen into the same temptations. It does seem as if I am slow to learn Thy ways and Thy laws.

I blush to recall my vows to Thee: never again to do what I have just come from doing, not again to stain myself in the same mudholes.

Yet O Lord, stained as I am, and conscious of my own weakness, I have no choice but to pick myself up again, to ask Thee to forgive me once more and make me clean again.

I thank Thee, O Lord Jesus, for the glory of the Gospel of the Second Chance. I would claim from Thee that chance to begin all over again.

Thou hast heard my prayer of confession. Now I claim Thy promise to forgive me and to cleanse me. From this moment I accept that forgiveness and that cleansing by faith, because I believe that thy promise is the "word of a Gentleman of the most strict and sacred honour."

And now I ask for Thy spirit to come into me like cool fresh air to revitalise me, to shock me into a new discipleship, to invigorate me for a new life in Christ Jesus, my Lord. Amen.

FOR SINS AGAINST OTHERS

Hear me, Father, as I make my confessions. I thank Thee that Thou dost receive me as I am—not as I pretend to be. I am so tired of pretending.

Forgive me for the times I have succeeded in deceiving my friends and loved ones, for I knew I did not deceive Thee. In sinning against others, I know that I have sinned against Thee. For hast Thou not said plainly that he who claims to love God, and yet hates his brother, is a liar?

Father, I know that in my ignorance I have cast a shadow upon many. I have stood in the way of their discovery of Thy way and Thy presence. O God, forgive me.

I have thought often of myself and my own needs, seldom of my fellow human beings and of their needs. O God, give me selflessness.

I have been unwilling to forgive others, yet have had the audacity to ask Thee to forgive me. I ask Thee for an understanding heart.

I have criticised other people in order to inflate my own importance. I ask Thee, O God, for a generous heart.

I have tried by reason and the twisting of my conscience to rationalise wrong into right.

There have been times when I told the truth only because I believed it was expedient to do so. O God, help me to love truth and honesty for their own sakes, that I may do right simply because I know it is right to do right.

I have sought the spotlight, yet am not big enough to stand in it. I want to be renowned for great deeds, and all the while am notorious for small performances.

I know that love for others is a gift of Thine. How much I desire it! Yet I cannot manufacture it. Increase, I pray, Thy giving to me, that I may have more love toward other people.

So may I go from this place to live my Christianity every day, in the things I shall say to others, in the things I shall do for others, in the way I shall live with others, that my own witness may be made to the love of Christ Jesus, my Lord. Amen.

RESTORATION

Father, I have lost the feeling of Thy presence. Yet deep in my heart I know that it is not because Thou didst leave me, but because I have wandered from Thee.

"All we like sheep have gone astray. We have turned every one to his own way." I confess that I have found that way hard and wearisome. My feet are tired of wandering. My heart is sick of being lost. I would return to Thee now and be led of Thee in Thy way, that I may walk once more with a sense of direction and a clear light upon my path.

O my Father, receive me—Thy prodigal child; prodigal because I have wandered in a far country, prodigal in my forgetfulness of Thee, prodigal in all the blessings I have taken for granted. Now, bowing before Thee, I acknowledge them all.

And now I arise and come back to Thee, my Father, knowing that Thou art even now running to meet me, placing over my shoulders the robe of Thy love, placing upon my hand the ring of Thy forgiveness, pressing upon me the kiss of a divine love that knows no limit—a love which loved me while I was yet a sinner—a love that brought Jesus to Calvary.

I thank Thee for that love; I thank Thee for this restoration. I thank Thee that Thou art still my Father, that I am still Thy child. Amen.

THE DEATH OF THE OLD SELF

Our Father, we believe that Thou wilt hear our prayers, that Thou wilt be sympathetic without coddling; Thou wilt have mercy without condoning; Thou wilt forgive, but not without a price.

Thou Thyself hast paid that price on Calvary's hill, and we, too, must pay a price if we would know Thy peace—the price of full confession, the price of real repentance, and the price of the crucifixion of the things within us that destroy our peace of mind.

Make us willing, Lord Jesus, to pay that price, remembering that without the shedding of blood there is no remission of sin, that without hard work there is no accomplishment, that without real effort there can be no achievement, and without the crucifixion of our old selves there can be no victory. Amen.

THE NEW MAN

" Therefore if any man be in Christ, he is a new creature: old things are passed away; behold, all things are become new." *II Corinthians* 5:17

I know, Father, that I must come to Thee just as I am. But I also know that I dare not go away just as I came.

Often I have known failure—failure in the moral realm, failure in ethics, failure in my attitudes, failure in my disposition.

I have confessed all these defeats to Thee, and Thou hast graciously forgiven me. Yet I know, Lord, that merely to forgive me will not suffice. For unless I am changed, I shall do these same things again. At last I know, Lord, that only Thou canst correct that within me which makes me do wrong.

Where I am blind, Thou must give me sight.

Where I fail to heed Thy voice, Thou wilt have to do something about my deafness.

Even where I deliberately choose to do what I know is wrong, Thou wilt have to do something about my will.

So, Lord, I acknowledge my total dependence upon Thee.

Make me over into the person Thou dost want me to be, that I may yet find that destiny for which Thou didst give me birth. For His help, who is plenteous in mercy, I give Thee my gratitude. Amen.

FOR NEWNESS OF LIFE

Lord Jesus, we come to Thee now as little children. Dress us again in clean pinafores; make us tidy once more with the tidiness of true remorse and confession. O, wash our hearts, that they may be clean again.

Make us to know the strengthening joys of the Spirit, and the newness of life which only Thou canst give. Amen.

THE GRATEFUL HEART

Lord, I pause to look back on the long way Thou hast brought me, on the long days in which I have been served, not according to my deserts but according to my desires and Thy loving mercies. Let me meditate upon the dark nights through which I have come, the sinister things from which I have been delivered—and have a grateful heart. Let me meditate upon my sins forgiven, for my shame unpublished—and have a grateful heart.

I thank Thee, O Lord, that, in Thy mercy, so many things I feared never came to pass. Fill my heart with thankful praise. Help me to repay in service to others the debt of Thy unmerited benefits and mercies. May the memories of sorrows that disciplined my spirit keep me humble and make me grateful that my God is no celestial Santa Claus but a divine Saviour. In His name I offer this sacrifice of praise. Amen.

FOR HUMILITY ON THE
MOUNTAINTOP OF LIFE

Lord, forgive me that when life's circumstances lift me to the crest of the wave, I tend to forget Thee. Yet, like an errant child, I have blamed Thee with my every failure, even as I credit myself with every success.

When my fears evaporate like the morning mist, then vainly I imagine that I am sufficient unto myself, that material resources and human resources are enough.

I need Thee when the sun shines, lest I forget the storm and the dark. I need Thee when I am popular, when my friends and those who work beside me approve and compliment me. I need Thee more then, lest my head begin to swell.

O God, forgive me for my stupidity, my blindness in success, my lack of trust in Thee. Be Thou now my Saviour in success. Save me from conceit. Save me from pettiness. Save me from myself! And take this success, I pray, and use it for Thy glory. In Thy strength, I pray. Amen.

FOR CONSISTENCY IN THE
CHRISTIAN LIFE

Lord, what is the matter with us that we are so fitful and moody, so changeful—one moment professing our love for Thee, and the next moment yielding to temptations that lure us away from Thee? One moment, cheerful, smiling, and kind, and the next, glum and surly. Lord, we do not understand ourselves! What strange creatures we are!

Yet we do not pray, our Father, that always everything should be the same, for we would get tired of unending sunshine, and long for a shower of rain.

We do not pray that our way may always lie on level places for then we would long to see a mountain.

We do not pray that always our lot might be favoured with pleasant strains of music, for then we would long for the ministry of silence.

But we do pray, O Lord, that there might be some pattern of consistency in our relations with Thee. Teach us how to maintain life on an even keel, that with a balanced life of faith and trust in Thee, and kindness and love toward each other, we shall not be at one moment up in the sky and at the next at the bottom of a well.

Help us to walk with our hand in Thy hand, knowing that Thou Thyself didst come down from mountaintops to walk in the valleys. So may we not give way to despair when we too must return to the valley, but know that the trail will wind up again.

But whether on the mountaintop or in the valley, may we

ever be aware that Thou art walking beside us. And if Thou art with us, what difference does it make where we are? In Thy name, we pray. Amen.

FOR CHILDLIKENESS

Forgive us, Lord, that as we grow to maturity, our faith is blighted with doubts, withered with worry, tainted with sophistication. We pray that Thou wilt make us like children again in faith—not childish, but childlike in the simplicity of a faith that is willing to trust Thee even though we cannot see what tomorrow will bring.

We ask Thee to give to each of us that childlike faith, that simplicity of mind which is willing to lay aside all egotism and conceit, which recognises vanity for what it is—an empty show, which knows that we are incapable of thinking the thoughts of God, which is willing to be humble again.

Then may we feel once more as do our children who whisper their love to Thee, who trace with chubby little fingers the pictures of Jesus in a picture book—those pictures that portray Thee, Lord Jesus, with a hurt lamb in Thy arms or a child on Thy knee. Help us, even now, to feel again like that, that we may be as loving, as trusting, as innocent, as grateful, as affectionate.

And as we are willing to kneel again as children, then shall we discover for ourselves the glory Thou hast revealed, and find the wonder of it gripping our hearts and preparing them for Thy peace. So shall we, along with our children, enter into the Kingdom of God, and know it, and feel it, and rejoice in it. In Thy name, who didst dare to come to earth as a little child, we pray. Amen.

FOR ONE BURDENED WITH WORRY

"Rest in the Lord, and wait patiently for him;
And he shall give thee thy heart's desires . . ."[1]

Father, teach me that, as Thy child, worry has no place in my life. I know that it helps nothing. I know that by worrying I cannot add a single cubit to my stature. I know that fretting overcomes no difficulty.

[1] From the oratorio *Elijah*, by Mendelssohn.

Often in the past, Lord, I have come to Thee with heavy heart and burdened life. And Thou hast answered my prayers and graciously lifted the burden from me. Yet with a strange perversion, I still refuse to leave my burdens with Thee. Always I gather them up—those heavy bundles of fears and anxieties—and shoulder them again.

Do now for me what I cannot do for myself. Wilt Thou break these habit patterns, reverse the direction of my negative thoughts, lift from me once again all anxieties and apprehensions.

Give me in their stead a calm and confident trust in Thee. Make me willing to live just one day at a time. May my heart re-echo to Thy promise that only as I rest in Thee can the desires of my heart be given me.

And now help me to do my part by placing a guard around my thoughts, by resolutely refusing to return to my old haunts of distrust. I thank Thee for Thy love for me and for Thy help. Amen.

TO LIFT THE BURDEN OF WORRY

Father, some of Thy children find life hard. It is for them we would ask Thy help now. Many of them are burdened with loads that they need not carry. Many of them clutch black burdens of anxiety and worry, when no child of Thine need be anxious. There are many who carry loads of fear when there is nothing to fear; many who make themselves miserable when they might be filled with Thy peace.

We ask Thee, O Lord, to teach us all how to live without strain. We have to confess to Thee that most of the things we have worried about have never happened.

Teach us the secret of living just one day at a time, knowing that each day brings with it so much joy that we cannot fully explore it, so many blessings that we cannot even count them—much less enter into them all.

So help us to be like children, content to live fully each hour as it comes. Then shall we escape the corroding care, the agonising worry that destroys our peace of mind, renders us unfit for happiness, and dishonours Thee. Then shall we be filled with joy and that peace which no circumstance can take from us. We thank Thee for Thy ceaseless bounty, for that joy and that peace. Amen.

FOR RELEASE FROM TENSION

" Thou wilt keep him in perfect peace, whose mind is
stayed on thee; because he trusteth in thee."

Isaiah 26:3

Father, we know it is not right for so much of hope, joy
and peace to be stolen from us every day. Yet sometimes
there seems to be no escape for us from the treadmill of
our daily lives.

We ask Thee to help us, to guide us into a finer way of
living. Check our impulse to spread ourselves so thin that
we are exposed to fear and doubt, to the weariness and
impatience that makes our tempers wear thin, that robs us
of peace of mind, that makes skies grey when they should
be blue, that stifles a song along the corridors of our
heart.

May we have:

The mercy of God to forgive us.

The strength of God to make us resolute to do His
will.

The grace of God to be kind, tender and affectionate
one to another.

The patience of God to believe in the ultimate triumph
of Thy kingdom on earth.

This we ask in His name in whom all peace resides.
Amen.

THE STRAINS OF LIFE

Father, many among us are tired, wearied with the strains
that life imposes upon us, the pressures under which we are
forced to live. We remember the days that are gone and
how harassed we were. We remember under what tension
we have lived, and we know that Thou didst not design
us to live like that. We remember the fears and anxieties
that brooded over us like a fog, and we know that no child of
Thine should ever be frightened by such spectres.

We thank Thee, our Father, for a moment like this,
when we may forget the sounds that have beat upon our
eardrums with relentless monotony. We thank Thee for
a moment in which we can no longer hear the chattering of
typewriters, the jingling of bells, the jangling of money on

counters, the whining of cash registers, the ringing of telephones, the noise of traffic.

And now, we forget these—and think only of Thee, Make within our hearts a quiet place. We release to Thee our demand to see what the future holds. We rest in Thee, content to know only Thy love and care in this present hour.

We release to Thee our struggle to cram too many activities and accomplishments into every hour. We rest in the knowledge that all of eternity, an infinitude of time, is Thy great gift to us.

We release to Thee the greed and over-ambition that has made us try to grasp too much of life too quickly. Help us to be content with simple tasks directed by Thee, done heartily and joyously as unto the Lord.

We release to Thee our impatience with other people and with circumstances. We ask Thee for the grace of patience and for the ability to relax when we must wait.

And now as we go back into the thick of life, may a quiet heart and mind attend us, to make straight our path, to open all doors ahead of us, to smooth the way in every human relationship. In Thy name, who art ever the Prince of Peace. Amen.

THE QUIETNESS OF PRAYER

" . . . in quietness and in confidence shall be your strength . . ."   *Isaiah* 30:15

Father, I ask Thee to take from me now all that does harass and annoy, all that has laid upon my heart burdens of anxiety and care. I thank Thee for the stillness of this time of prayer—this oasis in my busy day when I can relax before Thee, lay my burdens down, and hand over to Thee all my anxieties.

At this moment, I open my heart to receive Thy blessing, knowing that in Thy presence:
 the furrows are being smoothed from my brow,
 the lines from my face,
 the load from my heart,
 the doubts from my mind,
 the fears from my soul,
that I am at peace.

And now, I thank Thee, not only for quietness without but for Thy quietness at the heart of the universe and for quietness within. In Thy peace, I pray. Amen.

PRAYER IN PERPLEXITY

Lord, Thou hast said that our Father in heaven notes even the fall of a sparrow to the ground. Help us to believe, O God, that Thou art concerned not only with the rolling of the spheres in their orbits, but even with each of us, our doubts, and perplexities.

We remember all too well the bitter discoveries we have made when we have tried to run our lives our own way, when we try to steer our own craft. Wilt Thou come aboard, Lord Jesus, and set us a true course, for we grow weary of life's demands, tired of our own blundering ways.

We seek a clear light to shine upon our troubled way.

We ask Thee to give us clearer directions.

Where we have missed the way and wandered far, bring us back at whatever cost to our pride.

Take away our stubborn self-will, for we know that in Thy will alone is our peace. We seek that peace.

We pray in that name which is above every name, even Jesus Christ our Lord. Amen.

FOR PEACE OF MIND

Father, I know now, if I never knew it before, that only in Thee can my restless human heart find any peace.

For I began life without knowledge, but full of needs. And the turmoil of my mind, the dissatisfaction of my life all stem from trying to meet those needs with the wrong things and in the wrong places.

Help me so to live that my conscience shall not have to accuse, so that I may be saved the necessity of trying to mend that which need never be broken. I know that only then will the civil war within me cease.

May I be willing to have Thee with me in play as well as in work, knowing that with Thee I shall have peace and joy and no regrets. Through Jesus Christ, my Lord. Amen.

TO FACE THE FUTURE
WITHOUT FEAR

Thou knowest, Father, the things of which we are afraid—the terror by night, the arrow by day that takes us unawares and often finds us without a vital, ready faith.

We know that Thou hast not promised to surround us with immunity from all the ills to which flesh is heir. We only pray that when they come, if come they must, they shall find us unafraid and with adequate resources to meet them.

Give us a constant faith and a steady courage, that we may neither whimper nor in peevish petulance complain before Thee.

We thank Thee that Thou dost still rule over the world that Thou hast made. Kings and emperors come and depart. All the shouting and the tumult, the screaming hurricanes of time have not deviated Thee from Thy path.

Help us to remember, O Christ, that Thou art victorious—Christus Victor—reigning over all; that in due time, in Thine own good time, Thou wilt work all things together for good to them that love Thee, who are called according to Thy purpose.

May we find our refuge in that regnant faith, and so face the future without fear. Give to us Thy peace, through Jesus Christ, our Lord. Amen.

THE ESTRANGEMENT OF
A FRIEND

"So if you are offering your gift at the altar, and there remember that your brother has something against you, leave your gift there before the altar and go; first be reconciled to your brother, and then come and offer your gift." *Matthew* 5: 23-24

Father, Thou knowest the misunderstanding that has arisen between me and my friend. Harsh and thoughtless words have been spoken. I know that this rift grieves Thee, that Thou wouldst be far more impressed with a sacrifice of reconciliation on my part than with any vows of loyalty or material gift I could make Thee.

I dare not make this a prayer for Thee to change ——;

my friend is Thy responsibility. I know that always I must begin with *my* responsibility—myself and my own shortcomings.

In subtle ways I confess to Thee that I have used friendship to cushion and make comfortable my own ego. All too often I have sought my friend for my own pleasure and convenience; all too seldom have I thought of what pleasure I could give.

Thou hast asked me to love my neighbours and friends to the extent that I love myself. That, Lord, would be a lot of loving!

Enable me now to let all false pride go. Give me the grace of the outstretched hand and the open heart. Give me the courage that will enable me to go to ———— and be the first to say, " I have been wrong here and here. I am sorry. Forgive me." Help me not to take myself too seriously. Grant to me objectivity and a quiet mind and a sense of humour.

Go Thou ahead of me to fling out a bridge of goodwill, to cast down all road-blocks of misunderstanding. And bless to Thy glory and the happiness of all concerned this gesture of goodwill undertaken in Thy name. Amen.

FOR RELEASE FROM RESENTMENT

Lord, Jesus, Thou knowest me altogether. Thou knowest that I have steadily refused to forgive this one who has wronged me, yet have had the audacity often to seek Thy forgiveness for my own wrongdoing.

The acids of bitterness and a vengeful spirit have threatened to eat away my peace. Yet I have stubbornly rationalised every unlovely motive. I have said, " I am clearly in the right. It is only human to dislike a few people. This one deserves no forgiveness." How well I know that neither have I ever deserved the forgiveness which Thou hast always freely granted me.

So, Lord Jesus, I ask Thee now for the grace to forgive this hurt. Even now, I am divided about it, only partially willing to release it.

But Thou canst manage even my reluctance, my loitering feet. Take now my divided will and make it of one piece, wholly Thy will.

And Lord, I give to Thee this emotion of resentment

which clings as if glued to my heart. Wrest it from me. Cleanse every petty thought. Make me sweet again.

I dare to ask that Thou wilt not only forgive me to the extent that I have forgiven ————, but that Thou wilt bless ———— to the degree that Thou hast blessed me. For these great mercies I thank Thee, in Thy name, who gave me the supreme example in forgiving even those who slew Thee. Amen.

FOR MORE LOVE

Father, as I draw near to Thee in prayer, I am aware of the poverty of my love for Thee.

I have often given my heart to unworthy causes.

I have loved money and sought my security in it.

I have loved comfort and ease.

I have loved power and influence over others.

How strange it is that of all the things we humans love, our Lord, who is love and goodness and grace, should Himself receive so little love.

Yet I cannot manufacture the love I should bear Thee, even as I have not manufactured the love I feel for others. Thou art the giver of love. Except Thou bestow it, I cannot have it.

And so, my Father, wilt Thou give me the gift of love? Then I shall love Thee, and loving Thee, shall love other men—and compassion shall rise within me, warm and sweet.

But I ask not merely to love those easy to love. Help me to love those who are hard to live with. Give me a concern for the needs of others, not on the basis of barter or exchange —not love given for love received—but love given to the unlovely for Christ's sake.

Then shall my love partake of Thine, who dares to own me still. In the name of Him who is the King of Love. Amen.

FOR OUR FAMILY

Lord Jesus, we would thank Thee that Thou hast blessed our home with the gift of young life, for we know that through our children Thou wouldst remind us of God.

We do resolve, by Thy help, to honour Thee in all our

relationships—in our home, so that it may be Thy temple; in our hearts, where Thou dost love to dwell; in our place of business, that it may become an adventure in living our faith.

And now, Lord, we place every member of our family in Thy care and keeping. We think of —— and —— and ——. Bless them every one. Be with us all throughout this day—in our work and in our play. In Jesus' name. Amen.

FOR OUR YOUNG PEOPLE

Lord Jesus, we pray for youth in careless abandon, in love of liberty, and in joy of life, especially those particular young people whom we name now before Thee. . . . Help them to find that discipline by which life can alone be successfully lived, and character achieved. May they learn that just as steam is effective when contained in the walls of a cylinder, so will youthful energies be effective when controlled.

We ask Thee to:

protect them physically; throw around them the golden aura of Thy protecting presence;
be Thou their Teacher; be Thou their Guide;
send into their lives the specially chosen companions and friends Thou dost want them to have;
save them from any costly blunders that would haunt them down the years.

Give to them that joy and happiness that shall enable them to go out to meet life, bearing with them those lasting satisfactions which only Thou canst bestow.

We thank Thee, Lord. Amen.

TO CHANGE THE SPIRITUAL CLIMATE OF THE WORLD

Our Father, I think of all the pain and heartache, the tears and sorrow, the greed and cruelty unloosed around the world.

Help me to be an instrument of Thine to alleviate the pain, by this day:

returning good for evil,
returning soft answers for sharp criticisms,
being polite when I receive rudeness,
being understanding when I am confronted by ignorance
and stupidity.

So may I, in gentleness and love, check the hasty answer, choke back the unkind retort, and thus short-circuit some of the bitterness and unkindness that has overflowed Thy world. I ask this in the name of Jesus, who alone can give me the grace so to act. Amen.

FOR A CHRISTIAN TONGUE

"Whoever considers he is religious, and does not bridle his tongue, but deceives his own heart, his religion is futile." *James* 1:26—Moffatt

I need Thee, O Lord, for a curb on my tongue; when I am tempted to make carping criticisms and cruel judgments, keep me from speaking barbed words that hurt, and in which I find a perverted satisfaction.

Keep me from unkind words and from unkind silences.
Restrain my judgments.
Make my criticisms kind, generous, and constructive.
Make me sweet inside, that I may be gentle with other
people, gentle in the things I say, kind in what I do.

Create in me that warmth of mercy that shall enable others to find Thy strength for their weakness, Thy peace for their strife, Thy joy for their sorrow, Thy love for their hatred, Thy compassion for their weakness. In Thine own strong Name, I pray. Amen.

FOR LIBERATION FROM
MATERIALISM

Forbid it, Lord, that our roots become too firmly attached to this earth, that we should fall in love with things.

Help us to understand that the pilgrimage of this life is but an introduction, a preface, a training school for what is to come. Then shall we see all of life in its true perspective. Then shall we not fall in love with the things of time, but come to love the things that endure. Then shall we be saved from the tyranny of possessions which we have no leisure to enjoy, of property whose care becomes a burden. Give us, we pray, the courage to simplify our lives.

So may we be mature in our faith, childlike but never childish, humble but never cringing, understanding but never conceited.

So help us, O God, to live and not merely to exist, that we may have joy in our work. In Thy name, who alone can give us moderation and balance and zest for living, we pray. Amen.

FOR THE TRANSFORMING OF
EVERYDAY LIFE

Father, in these quiet moments we have a glimpse of Thy glory. Inspire us, our Father, to carry into the every-dayness of our lives all to which we aspire at such a moment as this. May our faith have feet and hands, a voice and a heart, that it may minister to others, that the gospel we profess may shine in our faces and be seen in our lives.

May we return to face the grind of the monotonous and the humdrum routine of duty with a new vision. Wilt Thou transform for us our common tasks and glorify them with a new light, that we may this week apply ourselves to them with fidelity and devotion.

Bless the homemakers, the mothers, and the servants who minister in the home, who maintain the sanctuaries to which tired men return.

Bless that noble company in white, the doctors and nurses. May their ministrations interpret the love and the pity of God.

Bless the teachers, often unheralded and unappreciated.

Bless all who are responsible for our transportation, who move us across this lovely land; all who in silence, and sometimes in darkness, toil while others sleep, that we may enjoy life and enjoy it more abundantly.

May Thy blessing rest upon all men who minister to their fellows. May each of us in our daily round come to know the joy of partnership with Thee, our Father in Heaven. In the name of Him who came "not to be ministered unto but to minister," we join these, our prayers. Amen.

FOR THOSE WHO SERVE

Lord Jesus, bless all who serve us, who have dedicated their lives to the ministry of others—all the teachers of our schools who labour so patiently with so little appreciation; all who wait upon the public, the clerks in the stores who have to accept criticism, complaints, bad manners, selfishness at the hands of a thoughtless public. Bless the mailman, the drivers of streetcars and buses who must listen to people who lose their tempers.

Bless every humble soul who, in these days of stress and strain, preaches sermons without words. In the name of Him who called us to be the servants of all. Amen.

PASTORATE PRAYER FOR
HEALING

There are loved ones today, O Lord, for whom we pray, and the prayers are even now being whispered before the throne of grace. We ask for Thy help without any hesitation, knowing that Thou art disposed to give even before we ask.

We thank Thee for askings that have been received, and prayers that have been answered. We are so glad that by Thy grace and mercy broken bones have been mended, weak and struggling hearts have been made strong. We thank Thee that pain has been removed; the sick have so often been made well.

Hear us as we pray now for some who need stronger hearts. Thou art the great Doctor who can do it. Wilt Thou strengthen the hearts of them whom we name even now?

We pray for some who are sick of tuberculosis, and while human skill can do this and that, and say wait and rest, we know that Thy skill alone can heal lungs. Hear us as we pray for that.

And we think of some whose eyes need to see. Lord Jesus, Thou hast not forgotten how to do that! Hear us as we pray for these miracles today.

And now grant to us that spiritual perception and faith that, having asked, reaches out to accept Thy good gifts.

Help us to keep our eyes on Thee, and not on symptoms. And grant, in Thine own time and Thine own way, a complete return to that health and strength which is Thy perfect will for Thy children. In Thy strength, who art the same, yesterday, today, and forever, we pray. Amen.

IN SICKNESS

" Hitherto have ye asked nothing in my name ; ask, and ye shall receive, that your joy may be full."
John 16:24

Lord Jesus, Thou art the Lord of Lords, the King of Kings. Thou art still the ruler of this universe. Thou art its Great Architect.

In the beginning, Thou didst design every part of it—from the twinkling of the great stars to the moulding of the petals of the wayside flowers ; from the colouring of the heavens to the tint of the butterflies' wings, even to this body of mine which is the Temple of Thy Spirit. Hear me now as I pray for Thy healing touch.

I confess that in my desperation and my need, I have wondered about the Providence of God. Forgive, I pray, this lack of trust in His power and in His love.

I acknowledge my unworthiness to ask Thee for any good gift. Yet I ask not on any merit of mine, but because of the claim purchased for me on the Cross.

Thou who didst Thyself explore all the vast treasures of pain on that Cross, bestow upon me Thy grace.

I have known Thee as the Saviour of my soul ; now I would know Thee as the Saviour of my body. I would find in Thee this day the Great Physician.

I pray simply and humbly, with a deep conviction that Thou canst still heal and that Thou dost want to heal me. As I discover Thy strength in this time of weakness, may I never forget Thy mercy nor cease to give Thee thanks as health returns. In Thy lovely name, I pray. Amen.

FOR THOSE IN PAIN

This morning, O Christ, bird songs pour in through the open windows of hospitals. There are pain-glazed eyes looking out to where trees—dressed in the green lace of spring —are eloquent of recurring life.

Thou, O Christ, art the author of this new life. Wilt Thou even now visit the sick as Thou wert ever wont to do? Lay upon fevered brows the cool fingers of Thy love. May those who suffer, whom we name now before Thee, feel Thy presence at their bedsides, and have the realisation at this moment of Thy touch, bringing to them new life and strength and health.

We thank Thee for the healings that have come, for the restorations that have been received, for many prayers answered. We thank Thee that Thou dost still heal today. We thank Thee for this, the sweetest word of the gospel message, that Thou dost come with healing in Thy wings.

We thank Thee that Thou hast heard and answered this prayer, born of our faith in Thee as the Great Physician. In Thy name, we pray, Amen.

FOR ALL PRISONERS

Lord Jesus, who didst come to liberate the captives, remember the prisoners, we pray, those locked up in jails, those confined to the huts of the chain gangs.

Release from the prisons of their own making all those who struggle with habits that bind them. If Thou wilt make them free, they shall be free indeed. Release them, we pray.

And Lord, remember the captives of illness, weakness, and pain. Loose them from that bondage into the heritage of health which is Thy perfect will for them.

Remember in Thy mercy the prisoners of sorrow who know not comfort, the prisoners of loneliness who know no solace of friendship. Thou who wast a friend to the friendless, Thou who wast a man of sorrows and acquainted with grief, remember them all most graciously.

Together we pray too for the peoples of other nations whose freedom has been stolen, whose liberties have been restricted or taken away, whose lives have known deep and dark shadows; for they too are prisoners, prisoners of human tyranny.

O God, let not the flares of freedom die out on the altars of their hearts that, having glimpsed that good life, they may not be disobedient to the vision nor forget the lustre of the freedom yet to be.

For these great gifts we ask confidently, knowing that Thou didst come to earth to free us from " the bondage of corruption into the glorious liberty of the children of God." Amen.

FOR THE LONELY

Lord Jesus, Thou hast walked earth's trails ; Thou knowest the nostalgia of human life. Thou who hast been alone in the wilderness bless now the members of the fraternity of loneliness.

To all who are bewildered, homesick, or ready to desert their post, give new courage. May they hear in the portals of their own souls the bugle call announcing the arrival of reinforcements.

May the friendship of Jesus of Nazareth be made known to them. May they find a welcome in this company of God's people. Wilt Thou guide and inspire them. Keep them from the mean and the low. Point them ever to the uplands of fellowship with Thee.

Transform for them their homesickness into new endeavours. Enable them to translate the affection of the heart into a new zest for living.

Direct our hearts that we may all be kindly affectioned one to another, abounding in love and sympathy, keeping back the unkind word, checking the hasty judgment, in all things being gentle and full of compassion in a world of hate. So may we walk softly before Thee and deal gently with one another, through Jesus Christ, our Lord. Amen.

IN TIME OF NEW BEREAVEMENT

Father, eyes blinded by the symbols of sorrow cannot see the stars. Even so, I, at this moment, can see nothing beyond my own grief.

I have been face to face with misery and loneliness in these days ; with the strangeness of life and death that takes away a loved one and gives no explanation ; with the mystery of a Providence I have tried to understand and cannot understand.

Thou, O Holy Spirit, Thou visitor in sorrow, Thou who art acquainted with human tears and broken hearts, sorely I need Thy help now.

Because my heart is sore, I have shut the door of my heart to my fellows, even to Thee. But I sense that withdrawal and the effort to dull my feelings is not the way toward healing. Help me now to dare to open my being wide to the balm of Thy loving Spirit unafraid of any depth or height or intensity of overflowing emotion.

> Thou hast promised to wipe away all tears from our eyes.
> I ask Thee to fulfil that promise now.
> Thou hast promised to bind up our wounded spirits.
> I ask Thee to fulfil that promise now.
> Thou hast promised to give us peace, not as the world gives but in the midst of our trouble.
> I ask Thee to fulfil that promise now.
> Thou hast promised to be with us alway.
> I therefore thank Thee that Thou art walking beside me every step of the way.

I put my hand in Thine, and walk on into the future, knowing that it will be a good future because Thou art in it. Amen.

FOR A FRIEND WITH A NEW GRIEF

Our Father, we think of that inner room of a family's sorrow into which only Thou canst truly enter.

Though all our sympathy goes out to these, our friends, we know that sympathy cannot bind up the broken heart. Only Thou canst do that. We ask Thee now to perform that gracious and healing ministry.

And help her who walked by his side—in this hour of grief and parting—to rededicate herself to Thee in a way that shall bring to her troubled heart Thy promised joy and peace.

In His name, who conquered death, we make this intercession. Amen.

FOR LONELINESS IN BEREAVEMENT

Father, I am only human, I need the touch of human companionship. Sorely I miss those I love who are with Thee.

I pray, O Jesus, that Thou wilt reveal to me unseen presences. Help me to know how close my loved ones are. For if they are with Thee, and Thou art with me, I know that they cannot be far away.

> Make real for me that contact of spirit with spirit that will re-establish the lost fellowship for which my heart yearns.
>
> Give to me faith shining through my tears.
>
> Plant peace and hope within my heart.
>
> Point me with joy to the great reunion.

But until then, enable me to live happily and worthily of those who are with Thee. In the Name of Him who is the Lord of Life, I pray. Amen.

FOR ONE WHO WILL NOT BE COMFORTED

Father, we join our prayers in asking Thy help for this one, who betrayed, still feels lonely. He has not even yet found the joy of Thy Resurrection and the sense of the presence of the one he loves who is with Thee.

Grant that he may feel her near; may somehow be persuaded that she still lives, that she is happy, that she still loves him as he loves her.

May such assurances come to all the hearts that need them today. We ask in the name of our Lord. Amen.

FOR THOSE WHO BEAR A LIVING GRIEF

Lord Jesus, Thou hast been despised and rejected of men; be merciful to the disillusioned, to all those whose hearts have been wounded.

There are some for whom skies are dark, whose future is uncertain. These are Thy children with nameless griefs, weighed down in the bitterness of sorrow, living sorrows that have no graves and cannot be buried. There are hearts heavy with suspense, who wait in the twilight of an excruciating uncertainty.

Thou art a God who knowest every sin and shame of our lives and who loves us still. Be gracious now unto all these. Make them to feel the strength and the power of Thy grace that grants the ability to endure.

But, Lord, we pray not just that they will endure. We ask that even as a grain of sand in the oyster shell becomes —by patience and the grace of God—a pearl, so may the troubles of these, Thy children, yet become tokens of loveliness to glorify Thee. May they learn through those troubles what a wonderful God Thou art! Then shall we lift up our hearts, for Thou shalt cause a new light to shine in their eyes and a lilting song to return to their jaded hearts.

We know, Lord, that at the last all the lost chords of earth will be found in Heaven ; all the broken melodies of our lives will be blended in the harmony and beauty of Thy glory. By this hope are we upheld and sustained ; in this hope we live. In the strong name of Jesus Christ, our Lord. Amen.

THE EVENING OF LIFE

Bless, O Lord, those who, nearing the end of their earthly pilgrimage, are sometimes tempted to wonder if they are forgotten ; those who sorely need Thy companionship.

Sustain and gently lead them as they find the outward man declining and the strength of the body growing weak. May they—each step of the way—come to know and to love the Everlasting Arms, come to know that the Lord is indeed their Shepherd and will not forsake His sheep.

May they discover the uplift of the Everlasting Arms and the grace of God to sustain them, that they may be renewed in spirit and mount up with wings as eagles, that they may run and not be weary, that they may walk and not faint.

Help them to see by faith the twinkling lights of that celestial harbour in which their moorings shall be cast forever. Strengthen their faith and joy as they look forward to that haven where loved ones wait. How Thou must love them! Be gracious, our Father, be gracious unto them all, we ask in the name of Jesus, our Lord. Amen.

THE CRY OF THE HUMAN HEART

Lord Jesus, Thou knowest the things that are trembling upon our lips, stirring in our hearts and along the corridors of our souls, walking on tiptoe across the cloistered spaces of our consciousness, conforming to the distant pealing of an angelus, looking expectantly upward, making prayers without words, breathing aspirations that have only wings.

Hear us, we pray Thee, as we call upon Thee for help, for strength, for peace ; for grace, for reassurance, for companionship ; for love, for pardon, for health, for salvation —for joy. Hear us, Lord Jesus. Amen.

ON THE THRESHOLD OF TIME

> ". . . I will fear no evil: for Thou art with me ; . . ."
> *Psalms* 23-4

Lord Jesus, as we look into the future, let no fears assail us. Help us to be as confident that Thou wilt be with us in the future as we know Thou hast been in the past.

We know that our Christianity is no insurance policy against trouble, but rather the guarantee that Thou wilt be with us in the trouble. That should give us strong hearts and confident faith. For so long as Thou art beside us, loving us, helping us, what have we to fear?

Bless each one of us every day as we try to live like Christian men and women. Where we are inclined to be satisfied with ourselves as we are, make us willing to be changed.

Give to us a more sincere kind of faith, a more virile, a more liveable faith, not alone a religion that smacks of Sunday, but the kind of faith that can be used on Monday and will not have evaporated by Saturday.

Hear us as we pray, standing on the threshold of time. Thou alone canst equip us for the tasks and the duties that are ours, that we may do our very best and quit us like men. In Thy strong name we pray. Amen.

CONFESSION—ON THE THRESHOLD
OF A NEW YEAR

Our Father, grant that in the days of this new year we may feel Thy love, the love that surrounds us, the love that will not let us go but will ever bring us back—back to Thy side, back to Thy will, back to Thy way.

In that way we would walk, O Lord. For though all we like sheep have gone astray, like sheep, we are tired—tired of missing Thy path and stumbling along paths of our own choosing. Like sheep, we would return to the fold.

We would come back to Thee, confessing that we are not proud of the mistakes we have made, not too proud of our record as we look back over the last year. We are conscious not of our triumphs and successes but of our failures. We are in no boastful mood, O Lord, as we look into a new year. We seek now Thy forgiveness for our stupidity and our obstinacy, for the blindness of our hearts, for the wrong choices that grieved Thee and subtracted from our own happiness.

Wilt Thou forgive us, Father?

Humbly and gratefully we open our hearts to receive that great miracle of grace. We thank Thee for the fresh, strong wind of Thy Spirit which comes to bring us refreshment, cleansing and perfect peace. Amen.

PRAYER FOR A NEW YEAR

May we who are pilgrims, conscious of life's varying scenes, learn by faith, our Father, to cling to Thee.

We know that Thou wilt be in the future as Thou hast been in the past.

We know that Thou wilt lead us on through all the tomorrows as Thou hast led us through the yesterdays.

We know that Thou wilt not let us go, even when we, in wilful neglect and indulgence, try to wander from Thy way.

As we set our faces toward the new year, we know full

well that it will bring many changes. The old must give place
to the new. Time does not stand still, nor the world cease
from its turning. Wilt Thou give to us the courage and
fortitude of mature men and women that will enable us to
stand upon our faith, as the spirit of the living Lord shall
give us strength. In Thy strong name we pray. Amen.

FOR THE COMING OF SPRING

We give Thee thanks for the loveliness of spring with its
promise of summer.

Bird and blossom seem to tell us of the possibility of new
life for our own souls. This spring day speaks to us of
beginning again, of new beauty that can come to reburnish
our own barren lives.

O Lord Jesus, may that transformation begin in us now
as we sit before Thee—penitent and expectant. Amen.

LINCOLN'S BIRTHDAY

Our Father, we think this day of one upon whose shoulders
in troubled times fell the mantle of great responsibility:
a child of the South who became a leader of the North,
in whose heart there lived that passion for union, that sense
of brotherhood and unity that neither war's alarms nor
the tides of politics nor the hatred of his foes could change
or diminish.

And we thank Thee that now our whole nation unites
in paying tribute to him who was humble before Thee.
We thank Thee for his understanding heart and whimsical
humour, and high resolve in all things to be on the side
of God. We thank Thee that the memory of such a man
is honoured among us.

And we do pray that something of the spirit that was in
Lincoln may indwell our leaders now, that they may see
as clearly as he saw that only right makes right, that only
as we are on the side of God can we hope that our affairs
will prosper.

We pray that Thou wilt raise up among us now other
men to walk as he walked, to talk as he talked, to rise above
the undercurrents of politics, so that they may see the country

as a whole and not be governed by pressure from this group or that, but may seek the common good and the will of God. In Thy name we pray. Amen.

GOOD FRIDAY

As we look upon Thy Cross, O Christ, filled with wonder and with awe at the love that brought Thee to it, humbly we confess that we have no offering meet for such a love, no gift fit for such a sacrifice.

Thou wert willing to go to the Cross so that men might forever be haunted by its sign, might return to the foot of that Cross to be melted and broken down in the knowledge of Thy love for us and all men everywhere.

When we see a love like that—the love of God yearning for the hearts of His children, we know that only love can respond.

We acknowledge, O Lord, that there is so little in us that is lovable. So often we are not lovely in our thoughts, in our words, or in our deeds. And yet Thou dost love us still, with a love that neither ebbs nor flows, a love that does not grow weary, but is constant—year after year, age after age.

O God, may our hearts be opened to that love today. With bright skies above us, the fields and woods and gardens bursting with new life and beauty, how can we fail to respond? With the clear notes of bird songs challenging us to praise, with every lowly shrub and blooming tree catching new life and beauty, our hearts indeed would proclaim Thee Lord, and we would invite Thee to reign over us and make us truly Thine own. May Thy healing love invade our inmost hearts, healing sorrow, pain, frustration, defeat, and despair.

May this day create within us a love for Thee of stronger stuff than vague sentimentality—a love which seeks to know Thy will and do it. So grant that this day of hallowed remembrance may be the beginning of a new way of life for each of us, a new kind of living that shall be the best answer to the confusion and to the challenge of evil in our day. This we ask in Jesus' name. Amen.

EASTER

"He is not here: for he is risen, as he said."
Matthew 28:6

We thank Thee for the beauty of this day, for the glorious message that all nature proclaims: the Easter lilies with their waxen throats eloquently singing the good news; the birds, so early this morning, impatient to begin their song; every flowering tree, shrub, and flaming bush, a living proclamation from Thee. O open our hearts that we may hear it too!

Lead us, we pray Thee, to the grave that is empty, into the garden of the Resurrection where we may meet our risen Lord. May we never again live as if Thou were dead!

In Thy presence restore our faith, our hope, our joy.
Grant to our spirits refreshment, rest, and peace.
Maintain within our hearts an unruffled calm, an unbroken serenity that no storms of life shall ever be able to take from us.

From this moment, O living Christ, we ask Thee to go with us wherever we go; be our Companion in all that we do. And for this greatest of all gifts, we offer Thee our sacrifices of thanksgiving. Amen.

MOTHER'S DAY

On this day of sacred memories, our Father, we would thank Thee for our mothers who gave us life, who surrounded us early and late with love and care, whose prayers on our behalf still cling around the Throne of Grace, a haunting perfume of love's petitions.

Help us, their children, to be more worthy of their love. We know that no sentimentality on this one day, no material gifts—no flowers or boxes of candy—can atone for our neglect during the rest of the year.

So in the days ahead, may our love speak to the hearts who know love best—by kindness, by compassion, by simple courtesy and daily thoughtfulness.

Bless her whose name we whisper before Thee, and keep her in Thy perfect peace, through Jesus Christ, our Lord. Amen.

Save us, our Father, from either indifference or unseemly revelry in this solemn hour, lest we mock those who lie in the quiet places they liberated from the scourge, and their comrades in whose eyes are the shadowed memories of the horrors they saw. Let us rather gird ourselves to finish the work they began, that God's peace may yet come to all our troubled world.

For the liberation of so many from the cruel hand of the oppressor, we give Thee thanks. As we were willing to make sacrifices in war, so may we be willing to make sacrifices to ensure a just and lasting peace. For those who are still in bondage, we ask a speedy liberation.

Make us aware of the responsibility that rests upon us to create peace in our own hearts, in our homes, in every association with our fellows. Teach us that righteousness alone exalteth a nation. Lead us; inspire us. Make us Thy people to walk in Thy way, that this land may become in a new and deeper way, God's own country. In the name of the God of our Fathers, who is still our God, we pray. Amen.

FOR GOD'S BLESSING ON A
MARRIAGE

Father, we know that Thou art the Author of Love; that the love which we bear each other is Thy gift to us, precious in Thy sight, precious in ours. Help us in the years ahead never lightly to regard that gift.

We know that the relationship into which we are about to enter is more than moonlight and roses, much more than the singing of love songs and the whispering of our vows of undying affection. We know that in Thy sight our marriage will be an eternal union. It is the clasping of our hands, the blending of our lives, the union of our hearts, that we may walk together up the hill of life to meet the dawn, together to bear life's burdens, to discharge its duties, to share its joys and sorrows. We know that our marriage will stand and endure—not by the wedding ceremony or by any marriage licence, but rather by the strength of the love which Thou hast given us and by the endurance of our faith in each other and in Thee, our Lord, the Master of our lives.

And now, as alone with Thee, we plight this troth: we do promise Thee, by Thy help, to be faithful and true to each other and to Thee who, having given us love and faith in Thee, hast given us all things.

We thank Thee that Thy blessing will go down the years with us as a light on our way, as a benediction to the home we are about to establish. May that home always be a haven of strength and love to all who enter it—our neighbours and our friends. We thank Thee. Amen.

THANKSGIVING—ON A
SUMMER'S DAY

We give Thee thanks, Lord of heaven and earth, for the promise of summer, for the beauty of this day—a day
> that shall ripen grain,
> that shall provide good things for the table,
> that shall make all growing things rejoice,
> that shall make more sweet the music of the birds,
> that shall make more beautiful the gardens which Thou
> hast planted and watered.

We thank Thee for the fertility of the land that encourages us to sow and to plant. We thank Thee for the dependence of the seasons, for all Thy sustaining providence by which men work today and harvest tomorrow.

We well know, our Father, that we are not worthy of Thy bounty, but help us to be good stewards of that bounty. We thank Thee for the endless delight of our lives on this lovely earth. Amen.

WORLD-WIDE COMMUNION SUNDAY

> " When I survey the wondrous cross,
> On which the Prince of Glory died,
> My richest gain I count but loss,
> And pour contempt on all my pride."

Father, it is a humbling thing to be died for. On this day we remember that Jesus Christ, Thy Son, did exactly that for each one of us. And He went to His death knowing full well how often we would forget His love. He went to His

Cross feeling the pains of the sins we were yet to commit, knowing that we should never understand the depth and height, the length and breadth of His love.

Father, let no pride in us keep us this morning from kneeling at the foot of that Cross.

Melt the coldness of our hearts. Soften the stubbornness of our wills. As we take the bread and wine, help us to enter into a new understanding of this great mystery that unites the hearts of believers all round the world.

So may we feel Thee closer in a new and wonderful way, knowing that we shall never be alone again, since He who loved us and died for us has sent His Spirit to walk always among us. In the name of Jesus, our Saviour, we pray. Amen.

THANKSGIVING DAY

Lord, Thou hast indeed been bountiful. As we look back over the years, how gracious Thou hast been, how tender Thy mercy, how warm and constant Thy love.

Create within us, our Father, that true gratitude that shall make this day of Thanksgiving one of rededication, when we shall think not of how much we can eat but of how thankful we ought to be.

So may we—all across this land today—act as recipients of God's richest mercy and bountiful blessing, as we share with others. May we, in gratitude, get on with the job of creating not only a nation but a world in which all men shall have the right to seek happiness.

Help us to make that dream come true in our homes day by day, in street and office and school, and so to live that Thou shalt be able to bless us and bless the nation for which we pray. In his name, who created us a nation, we pray. Amen.

A FAMILY GRACE—
THANKSGIVING DINNER

Father, we around this table thank Thee:
　　for Thy great gift of life,
　　that Thy love for us is not dependent upon any worthi-
　　　　ness of ours,

50

for good health.
that we know neither hunger nor want,
for warm clothes to wear,
for those who love us best,
for friends whose words of encouragement have often chased away dark clouds,
for the zest of living,
for many an answered prayer,
for kindly providences that have preserved us from danger and harm.

We thank Thee that still we live in a land bountifully able to supply all our needs, a land which still by Thy Providence knows peace, whose skies are not darkened by the machines of the enemy, whose fields and woodlands are still unblasted by the flames of war, a land with peaceful valleys and smiling meadows still serene.

O help us to appreciate all that we have, to be content with it, to be grateful for it, to be proud of it—not in an arrogant pride that boasts, but in a grateful pride that strives to be more worthy.

In Thy name, to whose bounty we owe these blessings spread before us, to Thee we give our gratitude. Amen.

EVENING PRAYER

Lord Jesus, we come to Thee for an evening blessing, to seal within our hearts the inspirations and memories of this day. We ask Thee for the blessing of
quietness for every troubled heart,
rest for every weary soul,
new faith and courage for all who have faced exhausting tasks this day.

We would rest now in Thee and find in this evening hour Thy stillness and Thy peace to bring us into quiet harmony with Thy will.

We give Thee thanks for
every challenge that this day has brought,
every new vision of God that winged its way across our skies,
every whisper of God that we have sensed in the beauty of Thy world,
every thought of God that came in quiet moments,

every need of Thee that brought us back again to Thee in prayer.

And now, our Father, grant us Thy benediction. Watch over us through the hours of darkness. Refresh us in spirit as well as in body as we sleep. Help us to face the tasks of tomorrow with steady faith and without fear, conscious of Thy presence and Thy guidance, knowing that we are Thine, as we have placed all our trust in Thee. We know that Thou art still able to keep that which we have committed to Thee.

And now may the love of God the Father, the grace of our Lord Jesus Christ, and the fellowship of the Holy Spirit rest upon us all and abide with us now and for evermore. Amen.

ON A WINTER'S DAY

We thank Thee, Lord, that there is no weather in heaven. Let not the dullness of this day get into our hearts or minds. May we be warm and cheerful, secure in the knowledge that Thou art still here, that no clouds can blot Thee out, no rain drive Thee away.

As winter blows her icy breath along the city's streets, our love goes out

to all who need encouragement,
to all who lack food and clothing,
to all who are cold and cheerless,
to all who long for home and friendship.

Help us, in our blessedness, to be more willing to share the good things of life. Give us generosity and that concern for others that shall mark us as disciples of Thine. Amen.

CHRISTMAS PRAYER

We yearn, our Father, for the simple beauty of Christmas —for all the old familiar melodies and words that remind us of that great miracle when He who had made all things was one night to come as a babe, to lie in the crook of a woman's arm.

Before such mystery we kneel, as we follow the shepherds

and Wise Men to bring Thee the gift of our love—a love we confess has not always been as warm or sincere or real as it should have been. But now, on this Christmas Day, that love would find its Beloved, and from Thee receive the grace to make it pure again, warm and real.

We bring Thee our gratitude for every token of Thy love, for all the ways Thou hast heaped blessings upon us during the years that have gone.

And we do pray, Lord Jesus, that as we celebrate Thy birthday, we may do it in a manner well pleasing to Thee. May all we do and say, every tribute of our hearts, bring honour to Thy name, that we, Thy people, may remember Thy birth and feel Thy presence among us even yet.

May the loving kindness of Christmas not only creep into our hearts, but there abide, so that not even the return to earthly cares and responsibilities, not all the festivities of our own devising may cause it to creep away weeping. May the joy and spirit of Christmas stay with us now and forever.

In the name of Jesus, who came to save His people from their sins, even in that lovely name we pray. Amen.

FOR OUR CHILDREN AT CHRISTMAS

Lord Jesus, who didst take little children into Thine arms and laugh and play with them, bless, we pray Thee, all children at this Christmastide.

As with shining eyes and glad hearts they nod their heads so wisely at the stories of the angels, and a baby cradled in the hay at the end of the way of a wandering star, may their faith and expectation be a rebuke to our own faithlessness. Help us to make this season all joy for them, a time that shall make Thee, Lord Jesus, even more real to them.

Watch tenderly over them and keep them safe. Grant that they may grow in health and strength into Christian maturity. May they turn early to Thee, the Friend of children, the Friend of all. We ask in the lovely name of Him who was once a little child. Amen.

THE DAY AFTER CHRISTMAS

O Lord Jesus, we thank Thee for the joys of this season, for the divine love that was shed abroad among men when Thou didst first come as a little child.

But may we not think of Thy coming as a distant event that took place once and has never been repeated. May we know that Thou art still here walking among us, by our sides, whispering over our shoulders, tugging at our sleeves, smiling upon us when we need encouragement and help.

We thank Thee for Thy spirit that moves at this season the hearts of men:

> to be kindly and thoughtful—where before they were careless and indifferent.
> to be generous—where before they lived in selfishness,
> to be gentle where before they had been rough and unmindful of the weak,
> to express their love—where before it had been taken for granted and assumed.

We are learning, O Lord, so slowly—life's true values. Surely Christmas would teach us the unforgettable lesson of the things that matter most—the ties that bind the structure of the family upon which our country and all the world rests; the love that we have for one another which binds Thy whole creation to Thy footstool, Thy throne. We are learning slowly, but, O God, we thank Thee that we are learning.

So may Christmas linger with us, even as Thou art beside us the whole year through. Amen.

FOR CHRISTMAS THE YEAR ROUND

> "O come to my heart, Lord Jesus;
> There is room in my heart for Thee."

Lord Jesus, we thank Thee for the spirit shed abroad in human hearts at Christmas. Even as we invited Thee at Christmas to be born again in our hearts, so wilt Thou now go with us throughout the days ahead, to be our Companion in all that we do. Wilt Thou help each one of us to keep Christmas alive in our hearts and in our homes, that it may continue to glow, to shed its warmth, to speak its message during all the bleak days of winter.

May we hold to that spirit, that we may be as gentle and as kindly today as we were on Christmas Eve, as generous tomorrow as we were on Christmas morning.

Then if—by Thy help—we should live through a whole week in that spirit, it may be we can go into another week, and thus be encouraged and gladdened by the discovery that Christmas can last the year round.

So give us joyful, cheerful hearts to the glory of Jesus Christ, our Lord, Amen.

PRAYERS FOR THE NATION
AND THE WORLD

AMERICA CONFESSES

Our Father, bring to the remembrance of Thy people Thine ancient and time-honoured promise: " If my people, which are called by my name, shall humble themselves, and pray, and seek my face, and turn from their wicked ways; then will I hear from heaven, and will forgive their sin, and will heal their land."

We—this company of Thy people assembled—would begin now to meet the conditions that will enable Thee to fulfil Thy promise.

May all of America come to understand that right-living alone exalteth a nation, that only in Thy will can peace and joy be found. But, Lord, this land cannot be righteous unless her people are righteous, and we, here gathered, are part of America. We know that the world cannot be changed until the hearts of men are changed. Our hearts need to be changed.

We therefore confess to Thee that:

> Wrong ideas and sinful living have cut us off from Thee.
>
> We have been greedy.
>
> We have sought to hide behind barricades of selfishness; shackles have imprisoned the great heart of America.
>
> We have tried to isolate ourselves from the bleeding wounds of a blundering world.
>
> In our self-sufficiency we have sought not Thy help.
>
> We have held conferences and ignored Thee completely.
>
> We have disguised selfishness as patriotism; our arrogance has masqueraded as pride.
>
> We have frittered away time and opportunities while the world bled.
>
> Our ambitions have blinded us to opportunities.
>
> We have bickered in factory and business, and sought to solve our differences only through self-interest.

Lord God of Hosts, forgive us! O God, by Thy guidance and Thy power may our beloved land once again become God's own country, a nation contrite in heart, confessing her sins; a nation keenly sensitive to all the unresolved injustice and wrong still in our midst.

Hear this our prayer and grant that we may confidently expect to see it answered in our time, through Jesus Christ, our Lord. Amen.

FOR GOD'S GRACE IN OUR HELPLESSNESS

We know, our Father, that at this desperate hour in world affairs, we need Thee. We need Thy strength, Thy guidance, Thy wisdom.

There are problems far greater than any wisdom of man can solve. What shall our leaders do in such an hour?

May Thy wisdom and Thy power come upon the President of these United States, the Senators and Congressmen, to whom have been entrusted leadership. May the responsibility lie heavily on their hearts, until they are ready to acknowledge their helplessness and turn to Thee. Give to them the honesty, the courage, and the moral integrity to confess that they don't know what to do. Only then can they lead us as a nation beyond human wisdom to Thee, who alone hast the answer.

Lead us to this high adventure. Remind us that a " mighty fortress is our God "—not a hiding place where we can escape for an easy life, but rather an arsenal of courage and strength—the mightiest of all, who will march beside us into the battle for righteousness and world brotherhood.

O our God, may we never recover from our feeling of helplessness and our need of Thee! In the strong name of Jesus, our Lord, we pray. Amen.

FOR THE PRESIDENT OF THE UNITED STATES

We pray, Lord Jesus, for our President. We are deeply concerned that he may know the will of God, and that he may have the spiritual courage and grace to follow it.

Deliver him, we pray, from all selfish considerations. Lift him above the claims of politics.

Fill him with the Spirit of God that shall make him fearless to seek, to know, to do the right.

Save him from the friends who, in the name of politics
or even friendship, would persuade him from that
holy path.

Strengthen and empower his advisers. Bring them, too,
to their knees in prayer. May their example and their
influence spread, that we, in these United States, may yet
have a government of men who know Thee, the Almighty
God, as their Friend, and who place Thy will first in their
lives as well as in their prayers.

Hear and answer, we pray Thee, forgiving us all our unworthiness ; cleansing us from every ignoble thought and
unworthy ambition that we may be renewed in spirit and
mind and heart, through Jesus Christ, our Lord. Amen.

FOR THE LEADERS OF THE NATION

Our Father, bless, we pray Thee, the leaders of this nation.
Strengthen the courage of the representatives in Congress
assembled—sincere men who want to do the right, if only
they can be sure what is right. Make it plain to them, O
Lord. And then wilt Thou start them out on the right way,
for Thou knowest that we are hard to turn.

Forgive them for the blunders they have committed, the
compromises they have made. Give to them the courage
to admit mistakes. Take away from us as a nation and as
individuals that stubborn pride which, followed by conceit, imagines itself to be above and beyond criticism.

Save our leaders, O God, from themselves and from their
friends—even as Thou hast saved them from their enemies.

Let no personal ambition blind them to their opportunities.

Help them to give battle to hypocrisy wherever they
find it.

Give them divine common sense and a selflessness that
shall make them think of service and not of gain.

May they have the courage to lead the people of this
Republic, considering unworthy the expediency of following
the people.

Save them from the folly of man-made schemes and
plans. Give to them the faith and the courage together to
seek God's inspired plan and, finding it, to propose it,
knowing that when it is God-inspired, Thou wilt open the
way for it through all obstacles.

As Thou hast made and preserved us a nation, so now mould us into a people more worthy of a great heritage. In Thy strong name we make these prayers. Amen.

PRAYER FOR AMERICA

Our Father, we pray for this land. We need Thy help in this time of testing and uncertainty, when men who could fight together on the field of battle seem strangely unable to work together around conference tables for peace.

May we begin to see that all true Americanism begins in being Christian ; that it can have no other foundation, as it has no other roots.

To Thy glory was this Republic established. For the advancement of the Christian faith did the Founding Fathers give their life's heritage, passed down to us.

We would pray that all over this land there may be a return to the faith of those men and women who trusted in God as they faced the perils and dangers of the frontier, not alone in crossing the continent, in building their cabins, in rearing their families, in eking out a livelihood, but in raising a standard of faith to which men have been willing to repair down through the years.

Thou didst bless their efforts. Thou didst bless America. Thou hast made her rich. Wilt Thou also make her good?

Make us, the citizens of this land, want to do the right things. Make us long to have right attitudes. Help us to be Christian in our attitudes. Let all that we do and say spring out of understanding hearts.

Make us willing to seek moral objectives together, that in united action this nation may be as resolute for righteousness and peace as she has been for war.

Bless those who bear responsibility. May they be led by Thee to do that which is right rather than that which is expedient or politically wise. Save us from politicians who seek only their own selfish interests. Illumine the minds of management as well as labour, that there may be an end to selfishness and greed, to the stupidity of men who are unable to find in reasonable agreement solutions to the problems that plague us.

Bless this land that we love so much, our Father, and help her to deposit her trust, not in armies and navies, in wealth and material resources, or in achievements of the human mind, but in that righteousness which alone exalteth any nation, and by which alone peace can finally come to us. This we ask in that name that is above every name. Thy Son, Jesus Christ, our Redeemer. Amen.

FOR THE GRACE OF BROTHERHOOD

We pray that Thou wilt teach us all how to live, that we may provide an example to all the world. Yet we confess before Thee the bigotry and the intolerance that plague us. We confess to Thee our disinclination to enjoy brotherhood, for we have withheld the spirit of it from many around us. O God, forgive us.

We remember that Thou didst bid us " to do good, to love mercy, to walk humbly with our God."

Give us such a vision of ministry that we can select for our philanthropy, for the expression of our love, these who cannot possibly recompense us at all.

Then only shall we discover what love really is, what brotherhood really means. Show us what Thou wouldst have us do today to make that discovery, we ask in the name of the Author of Love, even Christ Jesus, our Lord. Amen.

FOR WORLD-NEIGHBOURLINESS

Our Father, with so much bitterness abroad in the world —this poor bleeding world, stumbling from blunder to blunder, hollow with graves, hard with hate—may we who own the name of Christ, shed abroad Thy love.

We pray for a broader vision of the needs of all mankind, and a deeper compassion to fill those needs ; for a planting of the seeds of concern for all humanity in our hearts ; for a tapping of the wells of generosity.

Help us to live together as people who have been forgiven a great debt.

Help us to be gentle, walking softly with one another.

Help us to be understanding, lest we shall add to the world's sorrow or cause to flow one needless tear.

Help us to stand for what is right, not because it may yield dividends later, but because it is right now.

Help us to be as anxious that the rights of others shall be recognised as we are that our own shall be established.

Help us to be as eager to forgive others as we are to seek forgiveness.

Help us to know no barriers of creed or race, that our love may be like Thine—a love that sees all men as Thy children and our brothers.

God, help us all to be ministers of mercy and ambassadors of kindness for Jesus' sake. Amen.

FOR THOSE IN THE SERVICE OF OUR COUNTRY

We, Lord Jesus, are children of God. Yet we would not be the sons and daughters of men were we not sometimes fearful, did not our hearts often ache and harbour anxiety for those we love who wear our country's uniform, who serve her in distant places.

Yet we know, our Father, that the Everlasting Arms reach out across the world. We know that the shadow of Thy wing covers all Thy children.

We are persuaded that in that world of the Spirit in which we really live neither persecution nor peril nor sword shall be able to separate us from Thy love.

We know that the bonds of the fellowship of prayer are real. We know that at the throne of grace we are all united, that our souls can mingle with those we love on earth even though separated by tumbling sea and dreary miles.

So now our minds and hearts reach out to be in spirit with those whom we name now before Thee; to surround them with our love and prayers and hopes. For them we ask:

support in time of need . . .

strength beyond their own . . .

confidence that Thou art their Shepherd, that Thou wilt never for a moment forsake them . . .

Thy strength in temptation, that they may be kept clean . . .

the gift of inner peace, a serenity that no tragedy can destroy . . .

that knowledge of God that shall assure them of eternal
life, of peace and joy for evermore . . .

Thy gift of resoluteness in duty ; gird them with courage ; enable them to quit themselves like men who
have deposited all their trust in their God . . .

a determination toward love, not hatred, that the fruits
of victory shall not wither . . .

salvation of body and soul, and if it be possible, bring
them safely home.

We thank Thee that this ministry of intercessory prayer
has linked our hearts and bound us even closer to those
we love—closer to Thee and to them. May we feel Thy
presence, and see by faith that day when the love of Christ
shall live in the hearts of all men everywhere.

Hear, O God, not alone these prayers, but the unspoken
inarticulate yearning of every seeking heart bowed before
Thee. In the name of Jesus Christ, Our Lord. Amen.

IN A TIME OF NATIONAL DANGER

O Lord, when we, Thy children, are apprehensive about
the affairs of our world, remind us that Thou art in Thy
world as well as above and beyond it. Remind us that
Thou art not indifferent. For Thou art not a spectator
God, high and lifted up, serene and unperturbed. The
feet that were wounded are still walking the trails of earth.
The heart that was broken on the tree still feels every
human woe.

Thus shall we not feel forsaken, nor give way to hopeless-
ness. Thus we shall know that Thou hast a plan, and that
Thy will shall one day be done on earth, not alone by
those who love Thee and know Thee to be God, but by all,
not in one nation or two, but in all the nations of the
earth. Then shall every tongue confess that Christ is Lord,
and every knee shall bow before Thee.

Sustain us with that hope and encouragement, that our
prayer be not in vain when we pray " Thy Kingdom come."
Come it will, however dark may be the present prospects for
peace on earth—in the darkness of men's minds and the
hardness of men's hearts.

We do pray that Thou, O Holy Spirit, where Thou dost
find the doors of human hearts still closed before Thee, wilt
knock the louder and wilt, in Thy own secret way, prevail

upon the wills of men that they may do the will of God
—ere it be too late.

All these things we ask in that name above every name,
that name before whom all nations of the earth shall bow,
Thy Son, Jesus Christ, our Redeemer. Amen.

BEFORE A NATIONAL ELECTION

Lord Jesus, we ask Thee to guide the people of this nation
as they exercise their dearly bought privilege of franchise.
May it neither be ignored unthinkingly nor undertaken
lightly. As citizens all over this land go to the ballot boxes,
give to them a sense of high privilege and joyous responsibility.

Help those who are about to be elected to public office to
come to understand the real source of their mandate—
a mandate given by no party machine, received at no
polling booth, but given by God ; a mandate to govern
wisely and well ; a mandate to represent God and truth
at the heart of the nation ; a mandate to do good in the
name of Him under whom this Republic was established.

We ask Thee to lead America in the paths where Thou
wouldst have her walk, to do the tasks which Thou hast
laid before her. So may we together seek happiness for all
our citizens in the name of Him who created us all equal in
His sight, and therefore brothers. Amen.

A CHRISTIAN WORLD OUTLOOK

Remind us, our Father, that the people of France, Italy,
Greece, Germany, and Russia—the people of every country
in the world—are Thy people. Thou hast made them and
they are Thy children.

Some of them have rebelled against Thee, as have some
of us. Some have sought their own devices, even as some
of us. We are no better than they ; yet we are more richly
blessed and signally honoured. Forgive us that we are at one
and the same time so arrogant, yet so unworthy of Thy
bounty.

We pray for Russia. We thank Thee that Thy Holy Spirit
hast never ceased to work in that land ; that though they
know it not, the power of God is even now at work in the

hearts of the leaders of that great nation. And, O Lord, we do pray that as they look at us, they may see better samples of Christianity than most of us provide.

In the name of Him who created of one blood and one brotherhood all the nations of the earth, even Jesus Christ our Lord. Amen.

THE IMMIGRANTS' PRAYER

We give Thee thanks, our Father, that Thou hast guided us safely over land and ocean, that in Thy kindly Providence Thou hast permitted our lot to be cast in this pleasant place, that we are privileged to live in a land founded under God.

We give Thee thanks that this land was settled by men and women who came here, as we did, in order that they might live in the light of freedom, in order that they might worship Thee according to the dictates of their consciences.

Help us never to forget, our Father, that all the rights and privileges we enjoy here have blood on them, that every good gift was bought and paid for in human sacrifice. This goodly heritage is ours by choice and by adoption. May we never lightly regard it! May we ever be grateful to those who in years past have laboured and loved in order that we might have something to inherit. This we pray in humbleness and thanksgiving. Amen.

FOR WORLD PEACE

We pray for our troubled world, wandering in the excruciating twilight of an uncertain peace. In our hearts we know that this is no true peace—rather suspicion and fear, animosity and greed.

We ask that Thy Spirit will strive mightily with the leaders of the nations as they seek a formula by which the peoples of the earth can live at peace with one another. Impress upon their minds and hearts

that until we are at peace with Thee, we can be at peace with no one else;

that freedom can exist nowhere unless it exists everywhere;

Blessed are the pure in heart. Matt. 5:8

that the strength of this nation does not lie in armies
or navies, but in the integrity of her people ;
that peace is born out of righteousness—and nothing
else ;
that the trouble with our world is still—people ; that
peace is not possible until men's hearts—our hearts—
and the direction of our wills are changed.

Make us willing to be changed, whatever the cost to
our self-sufficiency, whatever the price of our insistence on
having our own way.

Wilt Thou reveal Thy will for America, that she may
now realise her destiny and place in Thy plan for the world?

O Father, grant that the promised day may soon come
when culture and learning, education and pity, shall again
light all lamps that wars have extinguished ; when all
wanderers can return to their homes and their little gardens ;
when "men to men the world o'er shall brothers be for
a' that" ; when all of us may be united in the high
adventure of building a better world. In Thy name, who
art the Father of us all, we make this prayer. Amen.

FOR A RENAISSANCE OF FAITH

Our Father, remove from us the sophistication of our age
and the scepticism that has come, like frost, to blight our
faith and to make it weak. Bring us back to a faith that
makes men great and strong, a faith that enables us to love
and to live, the faith by which we are triumphant, the
faith by which alone we can walk with Thee.

We pray for a return of that simple faith, that old-
fashioned trust in God, that made strong and great the
homes of our ancestors who built this good land and who
in building left us our heritage. In the strong name of Jesus,
our Lord, we make this prayer. Amen.

SHEPHERD OF THE SENATE

On January 5, 1947, a telegram addressed to Dr Peter Marshall was delivered to the door of the Presbyterian Manse on Cathedral Avenue in Washington. It read:

YOU WERE OFFICIALLY ELECTED CHAPLAIN OF THE U.S. SENATE JAN 4 STOP YOU SHOULD APPEAR AT THE OFFICE OF MR OCO THOMPSON FINANCIAL CLERK OF THE SENATE TOMORROW FORENOON AND HAVE THE OATH OF OFFICE ADMINISTERED TO YOU AND THEREAFTER OPEN THE SESSION OF THE SENATE WITH PRAYER AT 12:30 PM JAN 6 STOP
CARL A LOEFFLER SEC. OF SENATE

Thus—quite unpretentiously—Peter Marshall embarked on his duties as Senate chaplain. He felt strange, shy, and out of place that first morning as he hunted along the wide marble corridors of the Senate wing of the Capitol for Mr O. C. O. Thompson's office.

If someone had told Peter nineteen years before, as he was landing at Ellis Island as a quota immigrant, that he would someday be hunting for *anyone*'s office in the Capitol on official business, it would have seemed fantastic indeed. In fact, the suggestion of such a thing did seem fantastic to him on the morning when Senator Kenneth Wherry first suggested it.

In this month of January, 1947, there was a Republican majority in Congress for the first time in fifteen years. Two of the men spearheading the Republican conference were Senator Styles Bridges of New Hampshire and the Majority Whip, Senator Kenneth Wherry of Nebraska. Senator Wherry came regularly to hear Dr Marshall preach in the old red-brick church at H and New York Avenue, standing sentinel on its island in traffic. The New York Avenue Presbyterian Church was, moreover, Abraham Lincoln's old church. What could be more appropriate, these men thought, than to have its minister as Senate chaplain for the new Republican Senate? It was Senator Wherry who posed the question to Dr Marshall.

Peter insisted that he could not even consider such a post unless he had a most definite green light on it from the Chief. Several days of soul-searching on his part followed. Finally, he came to feel that God's hand was on this most unexpected invitation, and he agreed to let his name be proposed.

The quite unforeseen result was the first partisan fight on the floor of the Eightieth Congress—a matter of acute embarrassment to Peter.

An article by Harold B. Rogers in the *Washington Evening Star* of January 5, 1947, carried headlines: " DR. PETER MARSHALL ELECTED CHAPLAIN AFTER PARTY FIGHT ; Senate Democrats Lose Move to Keep Dr Harris in Post. The Senate late yesterday elected the Rev Dr Peter Marshall of the New York Avenue Presbyterian Church, as Chaplain of the Senate. . . ."

" During an extended debate over the subject shortly before adjournment, Democrat leaders contended that the chaplaincy should not be . . . subject to change with shift of party control.

" Republicans insisted there was no reflection whatever on Dr Harris, and said Dr Marshall had not been a candidate for the post. . . ."

When a reporter asked Dr Marshall if he was a Republican or a Democrat, he replied, " Neither. I'm a native of Scotland, and as I was naturalised after I became a resident of the District in 1937, I've always been denied the right to vote."

Peter never felt quite right about this brush with party politics, until that day came two years later when he was re-elected by the Democratic majority. In the beginning, because of these political machinations, his attitude was a little rueful about the whole business of being chaplain.

He became even more rueful when, within a few days, he had sized up the job for himself. It seemed to him that the Senators regarded the opening prayer as rather boring routine business. Ordinarily only a handful were on hand for the prayer ; the rest were still in their offices or in committee meetings. Moreover, Peter missed the worshipful atmosphere created in his church service for the prayer by the reading of Scripture and the prayer-hymn. The atmosphere was scarcely made more worshipful by shuffling papers, shuffling feet, coughing, doors opening and closing.

All this made Peter wonder at first whether he had been mistaken about his green light and was simply wasting his time. On most days he had to be up on the Hill at noon. Though the prayer itself was brief, the time it took to get there and to return to his office at the church ate into his working day. The Chaplain, he found, was also expected to act in the capacity of a pastor to his Senatorial flock—to marry and conduct funeral services for members of Congress and their families, to baptise their children, to visit them when ill, to counsel with them if they wished it. The Senate has always had a chaplain for these duties. The first one took office on April 25, 1789. Dr Marshall was the fifty-fourth chaplain—the first Presbyterian since 1879.

At the beginning, another difficulty troubled Peter. The Official Reporters of Senate Debate (the men responsible for getting all Senatorial discussion down on paper) requested of the new chaplain an advance copy of his prayer. This posed quite a problem, since Peter had never written out his public prayers. To do so seemed to him almost a denial of the reality of prayer, certainly of any heartfelt spontaneity. On the other hand, he did not wish to increase work for the overburdened reporters by forcing them to have to take his prayers down in shorthand and then transcribe them.

It was our friend Starr Daily who helped Peter to solve this dilemma.[1] Mr. Daily's suggestion that God could best specifically guide Peter's prayers for the Senate in the quietness of his study, enabled him to make the adjustment involved in giving up his usual extemporaneous technique.

Actually having to prepare the prayers in advance proved to be a fortunate discipline. It brought to full flower what *The New York Times* called "Dr Marshall's pungent phrasing . . . and tart morsels of thought." (January 11, 1948).

Then there was the matter of the length of the prayers. "It's quite obvious," Peter smilingly commented at home to me, "that the Senators appreciate my prayers in inverse ratio to their length."

Dr Marshall understood this and bowed to it. The result was that the longest prayer Peter ever prayed in the Senate —that of March 10, 1947, at the time of Mrs. Alben Barkley's death—took two minutes; the shortest, that which opened

[1] See *A Man Called Peter*, pages 246 to 247.

the Second Session of the Eightieth Congress—was exactly 36 words long and took a matter of seconds.

Peter's analysis concerning the inverse ratio of length to appreciation appeared to be correct. At any rate, it soon became apparent that the Senators were appreciative of his prayers. Soon after Dr Marshall took office there came to be a noticeable difference in the number of Senators present in the Senate Chamber in time for the opening prayer.

The fresh, spontaneous quality of the prayers seemed to give the Senators a lift. Never before had most of these men heard any minister speak in public prayer about their "sulking as children will" (January 17, 1947); about their being "confused . . . and at cross-purposes with each other" (April 3, 1947). They had never heard the matter of obeying God spoken of as "a forced option—like eating —" (April 23, 1947). They were a bit rueful and yet amused when their chaplain suggested that they "quit waiting for the other fellow to change his attitude and his ways . . ." and get on with changing their own (April 24, 1947). And when he spoke of "the stubborn pride that keeps us from apology and confessing fault . . . to one another" (May 1, 1947), and "of the balloon tyres of our conceit" (June 19, 1947), they marvelled at his realistic analysis of human nature.

The Senators liked the complete absence of sanctimoniousness in Dr Marshall. In his easy homespun colloquialisms they felt no effort to impress them with racy verbiage, but rather a man on intimate terms with his God, speaking to Him in a language that breathed an air of reality.

Many people (so they have told me since) whose daily routine included looking over *The Congressional Record*, acquired the habit of turning to the prayer first of all. Wire services like the Associated Press, periodicals such as *The Reader's Digest, The New Yorker,* and *This Week*, could not resist printing prayers like that of January 6, 1948, or that of May 14, 1947.

But there were far more significant results of these prayers than mere publicity. In his prayers, Dr Marshall emphasised one point above all. This was that the Senators could secure God's specific guidance, wisdom, and help. Increasingly, individual men began coming to their chaplain to talk about how this principle could be applied to various legislative problems.

One of the most appreciative members of Dr Marshall's Senatorial flock was Senator Arthur Vandenberg. Peter's usual daily routine was to leave his hat and coat in the Reporters' Office, chat for a few minutes with his friends there—Mr John D. Rhodes, " Scottie " MacPherson, and others—and then go on to the Vice President's office to greet Senator Vandenberg. The two men usually spent about ten minutes talking, then walked together into the Senate Chamber.

Perhaps the relationship of the two men is best told in Senator Vandenberg's own words:

" . . . he (Peter Marshall) was a very precious friend whom I came to know intimately during the past two years when I was serving as President of the Senate and he as Chaplain. We had a very beautiful relationship, a most intimate one, in which I am sure he gave his heart to me as I gave mine to him. I never knew a more rugged character. I never had a more delightful companion. . . ."

The Senator from Michigan was at that time in need of the quality of friendship which Peter gave him. Some of his colleagues in the Senate considered Vandenberg somewhat withdrawn and unapproachable. Perhaps it was because he had so much on his heart and mind that he sometimes gave this impression. In his private life there was the problem of Mrs Vandenberg's poor health. As the months went on, it became clear that her illness was very serious.

In Vandenberg's public life he carried a great load. In January, 1945, there had been his dramatic conversion from isolationism. In a courageous public statement he had said in effect, " I've been wrong. I now publicly renounce isolationism." It was a permanent conversion ; from then on he never wavered in his bipartisan leadership toward world responsibility.

In foreign policy, therefore, the record of the Eightieth Congress was an imposing one. It ended a hundred and fifty-two years of United States peacetime isolation. It approved aid to Greece and Turkey ; authorised ECA. It took the major inconsistencies out of the Truman Doctrine and placed it in the framework of UN. Both Senate and House members took their responsibilities seriously ; over two hundred of them abandoned vacations to trudge over Europe on their investigations. These events and other more everyday occurrences were the soil out of which grew Peter Marshall's Senate prayers. In order to re-create the setting I have interpolated between some of the prayers a few explanatory notes.

Peter had deep and honest admiration for Senator Vandenberg. Vandenberg, on his part, one day confided to Peter, using the Dutch nickname he had adopted, " Dominie, I've been a little disillusioned with preachers. You have restored my faith."

It would be presumptuous to try to measure or even to analyse the effect of Dr Marshall's prayers. The results are God's results. He alone can measure them. Only He knows how many of Peter's prayers in the Senate were specifically answered. Only He knows the truth about how much difference prayer makes in the affairs of men and nations. Only He knows to what extent Vandenberg drew inner strength and inspiration from his friendship with Dr Marshall during those crucial years.

God still works in mysterious ways. He uses a variety of instruments to make all things work together for good. At the very least then the Senate prayers were one of God's instruments, one of many appointed factors all weaving a pattern toward the good which God willed for those early postwar days.

The government copy of the Senate *Prayers* bore the following Foreword by the Hon. Arthur H. Vandenberg:

" Rev Peter Marshall was Chaplain of the Senate for two years while I presided as President *pro tempore* in the absence of a Vice President. Thus it was my daily privilege to greet him each noon when the Senate convened and to present him to my colleagues for his daily prayer. This duty swiftly became a precious privilege for me and this routine quickly became an inspiration. My Chaplain became my intimate and priceless friend.

" Dr Marshall was a rugged Christian with dynamic faith. He was an eloquent and relentless crusader for righteousness in the lives of men and nations. He always spoke with courage, with deepest human understanding, and with stimulating hope. To know him was to love him. His sudden and untimely death was a loss of major magnitude to countless friends in whose hearts his memory will long and vividly survive.

" I count it a rare privilege to be permitted this foreword to his Senate prayers."

Quite apart from the inherent value of the prayers which follow, Dr Marshall's Senate chaplaincy was a significant milestone in his own life and ministry.

When, as a college student, I had first heard him preach, I had been haunted by a sense of destiny for him. The call to go to Washington had only served to heighten that feeling.

Then, when Peter received the invitation to become Chaplain of the Senate, I found myself in the grip of an inner conflict. Nineteen months before, my husband had suffered a severe heart attack. Though he had made a fine recovery, too heavy a work schedule was as a Damoclean sword hanging over his head. I knew that the Senate chaplaincy on top of the duties of his regular pastorate, would greatly add to his burdens.

Even then, however, there was the deep intuitive knowledge that this new ministry was meant to be. It was part of Peter's God-appointed destiny. I knew that fear, even for those we love, is always petty, while a sense of destiny is a personal testament of faith. There could be little question of the decision ; faith must always triumph over fear.

Now in retrospect, I know how surely God led us. For January 6, 1947, when Dr Marshall first stood on the floor of the Senate to pray, marked the beginning of what was to become an ever-widening ministry.

It was at that time that the nation at large began to hear about Peter Marshall. Then on that dismal winter's day in January, 1949, when he left us so suddenly, it looked as if his ministry was forever cut off.

But God's ways are never our ways, and God had quite a different plan. Someday the whole story can be told— a fairy-tale sort of story, so incredible that no other explanation for it seems possible apart from the golden alchemy of a loving God.

Suffice it to say here that through the printed word Peter Marshall is preaching to more people today than he could ever have reached in a lifetime from the pulpit of any church. It would be a conservative estimate to say that two million people across the English-speaking world have read *A Man Called Peter* ; fifteen million more, in many languages, *The Reader's Digest* and the State Department condensations.

No longer can any one church or denomination or nation claim Peter Marshall. For in the six years since his death, his ministry has leaped over all boundaries to become a cherished part of the heritage of Christendom around the world. I'm quite sure Peter knows about all this, has marvelled at it, and rejoiced in it. In fact, it's exactly as he would have liked it.

Catherine Marshall

Washington, June 8, 1954

EIGHTIETH CONGRESS

MONDAY, JANUARY 6, 1947

The Republican majority in Congress was in an oppose-Truman mood. Peter Marshall was not an astute follower of politics. "My interest, if any, is in public issues, not party politics," he said in an interview. Nevertheless he caught the atmosphere and its spiritual causes immediately.

He knew that the spirit of both Republicans and Democrats would have to be changed if we were to secure the best legislation for the country.

He also knew that facing this Eightieth Congress were tangles far too difficult of solution for any human wisdom. Therefore Peter's great desire was to bring to these men an awareness of and receptivity to God and His will for the specific issues before them.

O Lord our God, if ever we needed Thy wisdom and Thy guidance, it is now—as the Congress begins a new session, standing upon the threshold of a new year, fraught with so many dangerous opportunities.

We pray that Thou wilt bless these men chosen by the people of this Nation, for Thou knowest them, their needs, their motives, their hopes and their fears. Lord Jesus, put Thine arm around them to give them strength, and speak to them to give them wisdom greater than their own. May they hear Thy voice and seek Thy guidance.

May they remember that Thou art concerned about what is said and done here, and may they have clear conscience before Thee, that they need fear no man. Bless each of us according to our deepest need, and use us for Thy glory, we humbly ask in Jesus' name. Amen.

WEDNESDAY, JANUARY 8, 1947

Eternal Father of our souls, grant to the Members and the officers of this body a sacred moment of quiet ere they take up the duties of the day. Turn their thoughts to Thee and open their hearts to Thy Spirit that they may have wisdom in their decisions, understanding in their thinking, love in their attitudes, and mercy in their judgments.

Let them not think, when this prayer is said, that their dependence upon Thee is over, and forget Thy counsels for the rest of the day.

Rather from these moments of heart-searching may there come such a sweetness of disposition that all may know that Thou art in this place. From this holy interlude may there flow light and joy and power that will remain with them until night shall bring Thy whispered benediction, "Well done, good and faithful servant."

So help us all this day, through Jesus Christ our Lord. Amen.

FRIDAY, JANUARY 10, 1947

Lord Jesus, Thou hast promised to give us the Holy Spirit if we are willing to open our hearts and let Him in. Make us willing now that things of eternal significance may begin to happen here.

We know deep down in our hearts that without Thy guidance we can do nothing, but with Thee we can do all things. Let us not be frightened by the problems that confront us, but rather give Thee thanks that Thou hast matched us with this hour. May we resolve, God helping us, to be part of the answer, and not part of the problem. For Jesus' sake. Amen.

MONDAY, JANUARY 13, 1947

Save this moment, O Lord, from being merely a gesture to custom or convention, and make it a real experience for each one of us in this place, as we call upon Thee for guidance and for help.

We have felt Thee near and beside us in the exalted experience of worship in church; make us now to feel Thy nearness in the business of the day—the Unseen Delegate, present and voting. Vote through these men, we pray Thee, O Jesus, that what they say and what they do may be in accordance with Thy will for this land that we love so much.

Thou hast said: "When ye stand praying, forgive, if ye have aught against any." Give us the grace to lay aside all bitterness or resentment we may be nursing in our hearts, lest their acid eat into our peace and corrode our spirits.

Thou hast said: "It is more blessed to give than to receive." Give us the grace today to think not of what we can get but of what we can give, that a new spirit may come into our work here, with a new vision and a new purpose, that Thou wilt delight to bless.

We ask these things in Thine own name and for Thy sake. Amen.

WEDNESDAY, JANUARY 15, 1947

Our Father who art in heaven, we acknowledge that Thou dost govern in the affairs of men. And if a sparrow cannot fall to the ground without Thy notice, how can we think Thou art indifferent to what we say and do here?

If this day Thou dost want us to do, or not to do, any particular thing, we pray that Thou wilt make it plain to us, for Thou knowest how blind we can be, and how stubborn, in our own intentions. We pray for Thy help in our thinking and Thy love in our hearts. Through Jesus Christ our Lord. Amen.

FRIDAY, JANUARY 17, 1947

O Lord our God, before whom one day we shall all have to give account, lend us Thine aid, that this day's work may be well pleasing unto Thee.

If there be any here sulking as children will, deal with and enlighten him. Make it day about that person, so that he shall see himself and be ashamed. Make it heaven about him, Lord, by the only way to heaven—forgetfulness of self—and make it day about his neighbours, so that they shall help and not hinder him.

Forgetful ourselves, help us to bear cheerfully the forgetfulness of others. Give us courage, and faith, and the quiet mind. Give life to our good intentions, lest they be stillborn. Bless us in all that is right, and correct us in all that is wrong. We ask of Thee this help and mercy for Christ's sake. Amen.

O Lord our God, we remember Thy promise that wheresoever two or three are gathered together in Thy name, there Thou art in the midst of them. We claim that promise this morning, and pray that each one of us may be aware of Thy presence, for Thou knowest our needs and how inadequate we feel ourselves to be in the presence of world problems and the challenges of this hour. If Thou wilt help us, O Lord, then shall we be better than we are, wiser than we know, and stronger than we dream.

In this prayer, we bring unto Thee the Members of this body, its officers and its servants, for Thy blessing; men who feel the weight of responsibility and the need of divine guidance; men who often are sorely tempted and who need the support of Thy grace. Bestow upon them the courage to do the right as Thou hast given them to see the right, and make it clear unto us all, for Jesus' sake. Amen.

WEDNESDAY, JANUARY 22, 1947

" Dear Lord and Father of mankind,
   Forgive our feverish ways;
Reclothe us in our rightful mind,
In purer lives Thy service find,
   In deeper reverence, praise.

Take from our souls the strain and stress,
And let our ordered lives confess
The beauty of Thy peace."

Deliver us, O Lord, from the foolishness of impatience. Let us not be in such a hurry as to run on without Thee. We know that it takes a lifetime to make a tree; we know that fruit does not ripen in an afternoon, and Thou Thyself didst take a week to make the universe.

May we remember that it takes time to build the nation that can truly be called God's own country. It takes time to work out the kind of peace that will endure. It takes time to find out what we should do, what is right and what is best.

Slow us down, O Lord, that we may take time to think,

time to pray, and time to find out Thy will. Then give us the sense and the courage to do it, for the good of our country and the glory of Thy name. Amen.

O Father in heaven, ere we become involved in the routine of the day, we pause to seek Thy help. Experienced in the ways of men, we know all too little of the ways of God.

But Thou knowest us, each one of us, by name and by our needs. Turn our wayward minds and hearts to Thee. Forgive the faults and failures of the past and set us free from them. Forgive, O Lord, our failure to apply to ourselves the standards of conduct we demand of others. Forgive our slowness to see the good in our fellows and to see the evil in ourselves. In our differences may we be kind ; in our agreements may we be humble, that Thy will may be done in us, and through us in our beloved land. For Jesus' sake. Amen.

"... when we give ourselves to lesser loyalties and spend our time and our energies in that which is less than ... the best ..."

The Congress was faced with decisions that would affect world peace for generations to come—what to do about China after our effort to back Chiang-Kai-shek appeared to be failing ; what to do about atomic control, the Marshall Plan for aid to Europe, grave labour trouble, etc.

Yet, at such a time, much discussion and effort were expended on issuing 3-cent airmail postcards on " good, stiff paper " ; a bill to recondition the vessel Prowler and return it to the Pomperang Council of the Boy Scouts of Bridgeport, Connecticut ; a bill to authorise Federal funds for fighting cattle grubs, etc., etc.

O Lord our God, before whom all our pretences fall away, who knowest our secret thoughts and our hidden fears, bless us this day with Thy Spirit and help us to discharge our duties faithfully and well. Ever sensitive to the hurting of our own feelings, may we be sensitive also to our grieving of Thy Holy Spirit when we give ourselves to the lesser loyalties and spend our time and our energies in that which is less than the highest and the best.

We pray for the President of the United States, the members of the Cabinet, the representatives of the people, the judges of the land, and all those in authority, that it may please Thee so to rule their hearts that they may rightly use the trust committed to them for the good of all people.

Raise up among us, we pray Thee, fearless men who know that only in the doing of Thy will can we find our peace. So make it plain to us this day, and give us the courage to do it. All this we beg for Jesus Christ's sake. Amen.

WEDNESDAY, JANUARY 29, 1947

O God of Truth, who alone canst lead men into the truth that is freedom and joy, be Thou our teacher as we seek to find the way of life in times that bewilder and challenge.

Teach us better to know ourselves, that, knowing our weaknesses, we may be on guard. Teach us better to understand other people, that we may view their shortcomings with charity, their virtues with appreciation, and their kindness to us with gratitude.

Be with Thy servants in this place, in all things great and small, so that small things become great and great things become possible. Father of mercies, bless their loved ones and their families, and make their homes sanctuaries of love and peace where they may find spiritual resources for the strain and pressure of their duties here.

Give us now Thy spirit to guide and direct our thinking, that when the day's work is over we may merit Thy "Well done." Through Jesus Christ our Lord. Amen.

FRIDAY, JANUARY 31, 1947

Almighty God, creator of all things, giver of every good and perfect gift, hear us this day as we seek Thy blessing upon our deliberations.

We acknowledge before Thee our shortcomings, our selfishness, our smugness, and our pride. Forgive us wherein we have come short of Thy will for us and for our Nation.

Create within us clean hearts, and renew right spirits, that we may do better and be better. Forgive us our forgetfulness of the world's sore need and our contentment with things as they are.

Hear us when we pray for all those in places of influence and authority, that they may do right. Guide those who lead us; and touch Thy servants with Thy Holy Spirit, that their faith may be revived, their hope renewed, and their vision made clear and challenging. Give to them the conviction that with Thy help all things are possible—even the most difficult things that baffle us now. God forbid that any of us here should add to the problems of the hour, but rather resolve, by Thy help, to become part of the answer. So help us, God, for Jesus' sake. Amen.

MONDAY, FEBRUARY 3, 1947

"Amid all the pressures brought upon them. . . ."

Much of the pressure during this month of February was brought by powerful industrialists who had descended on Washington to demand high tariffs. Production capacity of the Nation had been increased by World War II, and the United States was in a position to supply the rest of the world with many commodities, and thus lead the way to recovery. But if economic nationalism were allowed to continue, other countries would have no chance at all to get on their feet.

Our Father, as we come before the Throne of Grace this day, we would not weary Thee with our constant begging. We would not be like petulant children seeking diplomas without study, or wages without work.

We thank Thee for lessons to learn and for work to do. May we apply ourselves to both.

As Thy servants here sincerely seek to do right, make it plain to them. Knowing that criticism will come, help them to take from it what is helpful and to forgive what is unjust and unkind. Amid all the pressures brought upon them, may they ever hear Thy still small voice and follow Thy guidance for the good of all the people, that Thy will may be done in this Nation, through these Thy servants. For Jesus' sake. Amen.

WEDNESDAY, FEBRUARY 5, 1947

Our Father, in the midst of the complicated situations of life and the unsolved problems of the world, deliver Thy servants from any sense of futility. Let them feel the support of the prayers of hosts of true patriots throughout this land and, above all, the uplift of the Everlasting Arms.

Cause them to understand that God's power has never been obstructed by difficulties, nor His love limited by the confusion of human plans. May the very failure of man's best resources impel us toward the resources of God.

Cleanse our hearts of selfishness. Grant that all questions immediately before us may be made so plain that we shall have no forebodings as we make our decision, nor vain regrets after it is made. For Jesus' sake. Amen.

FRIDAY, FEBRUARY 7, 1947

Forgive us, O God, for all our boasting and our presumptuous sins of pride and arrogance, for these are days that humble us.

By Thy grace we become more and more aware of our limitations and our weaknesses.

Let us not mistake humility for an inferiority complex, but help us to understand that with the proud and the self-sufficient Thou canst do nothing until Thou hast brought them to their knees.

We need Thy help, our Father, and we seek it humbly. We want to do right, and to be right; so start us in the right way, for Thou knowest that we are very hard to turn. Shed forth Thy grace upon us, O Lord, that each man here may say, " I can do all things through Christ which strengthened me." We ask it in His name. Amen.

MONDAY, FEBRUARY 10, 1947

O Lord teach us to number our days that we may apply our hearts unto wisdom. Time is short, and no one of us knows how little time he has left. May we be found using wisely our time, our talents, and our strength.

Break to us this day the bread of life. Our hearts are hungry, as are the hearts of people everywhere. Save us from thinking, even for a moment, that we can feed our souls on things. Save us from the vain delusion that the piling up of wealth or comforts can satisfy.

Save these, Thy servants, the chosen of the people, from the tyranny of the non-essential, from the weary round of that which saps strength, frays nerves, shortens life, and adds nothing to their usefulness to Thee and to this Nation. Help them to give themselves to the important and to recognise the trivial when they see it. Give them the courage to say "No" to everything that makes it more difficult to say "Yes" to Thee. For Jesus' sake. Amen.

TUESDAY, FEBRUARY 11, 1947

We thank Thee, Almighty God, for the rich heritage of this good land, for the evidences of Thy favour in the past, and for the Hand that hath made and preserved us a nation.

We thank Thee for the men and women who, by blood and sweat, by toil and tears, forged on the anvil of their own sacrifice all that we hold dear. May we never lightly esteem what they obtained at a great price. Grateful for rights and privileges, may we be conscious of duties and obligations.

On this day we thank Thee for the inspiration that breathes in the memory of Abraham Lincoln, and we pray that something of the spirit that was his may be ours today. Like him, may we be more concerned that we are on Thy side, than that Thou art on ours. In our hearts may there be, as there was in his, "malice toward none and charity for all"; that we may, together, with Thy blessing and help, "bind up the nation's wounds, and do all which may achieve and cherish a just and lasting peace among ourselves and with all nations." Through Jesus Christ our Lord. Amen.

FRIDAY, FEBRUARY 14, 1947

O Thou Great Architect of the Universe, whom, by the revelation of Thy Son our Lord, we may address as our Father, help us to understand what that means. As we are now united in our praying, so may we be united in our working, that, as a team, we may be doing together the will of our Father, who is not a God of any one part, of any one nation, or of any one race.

Open our eyes that we may discern what God is doing, and our ears that we may hear what God is saying. And then, O God, give us all we need to take due notice and to govern ourselves accordingly. We ask these things in the strong name of Jesus Christ our Lord. Amen.

MONDAY, FEBRUARY 17, 1947

O Lord of our life, we would know Thee better, that we might love Thee more, and thus be more useful to our fellow men. Make us hungry for Thy spirit and Thy power. Let Thy grace come upon us that the will of our God may be known to us and done through us.

Let us not break faith with any of yesterday's promises nor leave unrepaired any of yesterday's wrongs. Show us what we can do to make this world a better place for men to live in, that the down payment made by 300,000 of our men may not have been made in vain.

May the urgency of the world's need remind us that promises do not feed the hungry nor resolutions give them shelter. May we be willing to act when Thou shalt show us what to do. We join our hearts in this prayer for Thy guidance. In the name of Jesus Christ our Lord. Amen.

WEDNESDAY, FEBRUARY 19, 1947

Our Father in heaven, we pray for the Members of this body in their several responsibilities. Help them in their offices, in committees, and above all, as they meet here in legislative session.

May they never forget that what is said and done here is not done in a corner, but always under Thy scrutiny. May they feel the weight of their responsibility before Thee, and remember the influence of a good example, that all who come to this place may have a stronger faith in government of the people, by the people, for the people.

May the Senators so speak and act that all who wait upon them may be inspired, rather than disillusioned by what they see and hear and are asked to do. Lord Jesus, make

Thyself real to these men, that each may feel Thee sitting beside him, and hear Thy voice, and win Thine approval in all things. So help them, God, for Jesus' sake. Amen.

FRIDAY, FEBRUARY 21, 1947

This was the World Day of Prayer, first observed in the year 1887.

We recognise, our Father, as George Washington saw so clearly that, " no people can be bound to acknowledge and adore the Invisible Hand which conducts the affairs of men more than those of the United States. Every step by which they have advanced to the character of an independent nation seems to have been distinguished by some token of providential agency."

Believing that the Hand that hath brought us thus far will not forsake us now, but if we are willing will lead us on into further inspiration and service to all mankind, we would join our prayers this day with those of Christian women all over the world in this day of prayer.

With so many souls united in intercession for our own beloved country and for all mankind, may there come an outpouring of Thy Spirit into our hearts and minds that we shall feel it and all men may know it. " Lift us above unrighteous anger and mistrust, into faith and hope and charity, by a simple and steadfast reliance on Thy sure will."

We pray for some evidence in what is said and done here that Thou hast been permitted a vote, and that these men have yielded their lives to Thee. In Jesus' name. Amen.

MONDAY, FEBRUARY 24, 1947

Our Father in heaven, we know that Thou canst see the hidden things in every heart. If our intentions are good, help us to make them live in good deeds. If what we intend or desire makes us uncomfortable in Thy presence, take it from us, and give us the spirit we ought to have that we may do what we ought to do. For Jesus' sake. Amen.

WEDNESDAY, FEBRUARY 26, 1947

With all the resources of an infinite God available to them that ask Thee, forgive us, O Lord, for our lack of faith that begs for pennies when we could write cheques for millions, that strikes a match when we could have the sun.

Give to us the faith to believe that there is no problem before us that Thy wisdom cannot solve. As Thou hast guided men in the past, so guide these men today. At every desk may there be a whisper of Thy counsel. Help our leaders to weight their words, that their words may carry weight and, what is more, the echo of Thy will, for Jesus' sake. Amen.

FRIDAY, FEBRUARY 28, 1947

Give to us open minds, O God, minds ready to receive and to welcome such new light of knowledge as it is Thy will to reveal. Let not the past ever be so dear to us as to set a limit to the future. Give us the courage to change our minds when that is needed. Let us be tolerant of the thoughts of others, for we never know in what voice Thou wilt speak.

Wilt Thou keep our ears open to Thy voice and make us a little more deaf to whispers of men who would persuade us from our duty, for we know in our hearts that only in Thy will is our peace and the prosperity of our land. We pray in the lovely name of Jesus. Amen.

MONDAY, MARCH 3, 1947

" . . . help us to share what Thou hast given . . ."

Much of Europe was facing starvation. Critics of the Administration thought that the programme of exporting $3 billion worth of food (10 per cent of our food stocks, 33⅓ per cent of our total production) would impoverish us.

But Peter Marshall felt that the 10 per cent was merely a " tithe " of our food riches, and that God would abundantly bless the nation for this sharing. So it proved to be. We had a bumper wheat crop that year.

Lord God of Heaven, who hath so lavishly blessed this our beloved land, keep us humble. Forgive our boasting and our pride, and help us to share what Thou hast given. Impress us with a sense of responsibility, and remind us, lest we become filled with conceit, that one day a reckoning will be required of us.

Sanctify our love of our country, that our boasting may be turned into humility and our pride into a ministry to all men everywhere. Make America Thy servant, Thy chosen channel of blessing to all lands, lest we be cast out and our place be given to another. Make this God's own country by making us willing to live like God's people. We ask these things in the name of Jesus Christ our Lord. Amen.

WEDNESDAY, MARCH 5, 1947

Gen. George C. Marshall, then Secretary of State, was about to leave for Moscow to attend the Conference on Peace Treaties with Germany and Austria.

Our Father, we know that we, by ourselves, are not sufficient for these days and for problems greater than the measure of our best wisdom.

We pray that Thou wilt grant safe journey to our Secretary of State as he carries the hopes and the prayers of this Nation to the conference across the sea. A soldier himself, may he remember the price that was paid by millions for this opportunity, and may we, who pray for the success of the mission, be willing to pay the price for peace.

We believe, O Lord, that Thou wilt be present, with the marks of the nails in Thy hands, to lead them, and bless them, if they will receive Thy spirit.

May the ministers be aware of the Unseen Delegate. May Thy Spirit move them, that there may be concession without coercion and conciliation without compromise. May they, who represent us, represent Thee and, in Thy Spirit, be courageous enough to begin anew, fearless enough to admit mistakes, and loving enough to forgive others. May we have the courage to apply what we applaud, to the end that we may help to establish Thy way of life for the people of the world. So may we all do the best we can, by Thy help, and be willing to leave the issue in Thy hands, through Jesus Christ our Lord. Amen.

O Thou Holy Spirit, who hast promised to lead us into all truth, prepare our hearts and minds for the business of this day, that we may behave with true courtesy and honour.

Compel us to be just and honest in our dealings.

Let our motives be above suspicion.

Let our word be our bond.

Save us from the fallacy of depending upon our personality, or ingenuity, or position to solve our problems.

Since Thou hast the answers, make us willing to listen to Thee, that we may vote on God's side, and that God's will may be done in us. Through Jesus Christ our Lord. Amen.

Mrs Alben W. Barkley, wife of Senator Barkley (Kentucky), Minority Leader, had died in Washington.

Our Father, as we come into Thy presence this morning, we are saddened by the announcement of the great loss and bereavement sustained by one of the most distinguished Members of this body. Our sympathy goes out to him, deep and tender, as we stand at his side sharing his sorrow as far as friends may, and joining our prayers that he may feel even now the Everlasting Arms upholding him and Thy grace and Thy love sustaining him in this dark hour.

We give Thee thanks for his constant devotion, for the courage and the fidelity to duty that has marked these last years when he was called upon by Thy strange and mysterious providence to walk a hard road; and we give Thee thanks for the beauty and inspiration that his helpmeet provided in the difficult experiences they shared together.

We thank Thee for her charm and for the winsome beauty of her life and spirit, and we pray that Thy grace may be sufficient now for him who was her partner and for the members of the family who mourn her going.

We thank Thee for the hope Thou hast given us that There will come a day when the lost chords of life may be found again in that happy land, and all that is dark and mysterious now shall be revealed and its purposes made plain.

We pray that in this great sorrow, shared by each Member of this body, we may be drawn closer to each other in true comradeship and fellowship. May sympathy unite our hearts to each other and bind us to Thee, who dost mark our tears and hast promised to wipe them away.

So may Thy blessing be upon our brother now and upon all who are with him in the fraternity of sorrow, that their faith may be strengthened and their hope made bright and triumphant. Through Jesus Christ our Lord. Amen.

WEDNESDAY, MARCH 12, 1947

Almighty Father of the universe, we come to Thee, conscious of our own shortcomings but with confidence and composure, knowing that, having put our trust in Thee, our faith is well founded.

May we tolerate nothing in our personal living which, if multiplied, would weaken our Nation. Teach us that our country is no better than its citizens and no stronger than those in whom it puts its trust.

So may we see ourselves as Thou dost see us, that being ashamed we may seek forgiveness, and knowing our weaknesses may accept Thy strength. With Thy blessing upon us, we need not fear decisions nor hesitate to act. So use us, guide us, and act through us, we ask in Jesus' name and for His sake. Amen.

FRIDAY, MARCH 14, 1947

God of our fathers and our God, in the gloom of this troubled hour, disclose the brightness of Thy presence and revive within us the hope of our faith.

Deliver us from discouragement, and when we feel most helpless, make us turn to Thee for the answers Thou hast for every question. Enable us to see issues clearly, before crisis clouds them, and help us to choose the good course, lest relying upon our own wisdom we have to choose between evils.

Give us the boldness of a faith that has conviction as well

as sentiment, and take from us all fear save that of failing to do Thy will. We ask in the name of Him who died for all men, even Jesus Christ our Lord. Amen.

MONDAY, MARCH 17, 1947

Lord Jesus, we turn in confidence unto Thee, since Thou wast tempted in all points like as we are, and yet without sin. Help us, that we may obtain victory over our temptations. We feel ashamed that we have so little power in our lives and so often fall at the same old hurdles. Sometimes we grow discouraged and filled with doubts when we see so little evidence of growth in grace, in faith, and in spiritual perception.

We know that we are not what we ought to be; and we know that we are not yet what we will be; but we thank Thee that we are not what we once were. For whatever progress Thou hast made with us we give Thee thanks, and by Thy grace we are kept from despair. Help us to remember that they that wait upon the Lord shall renew their strength. May we wait and be made strong. Through Jesus Christ our Lord. Amen.

TUESDAY, MARCH 18, 1947

Our Father in heaven, who dost know every secret of our hearts—all that we fear, all that we hope, and all of which we are ashamed—in this moment of confusion, as each man looks into his own heart and mind, have mercy upon us all, and make us clean inside, that in all we do today we may behave with true courtesy and honour. Let us be kind in our criticism of others, and slow to judge, knowing that we ourselves must one day be judged.

We pray for a new spirit to come upon us that we may be able to do more and better work. Through Jesus Christ our Lord. Amen.

WEDNESDAY, MARCH 19, 1947

Lord Jesus, Thou who art the way, the truth, and the life, hear us as we pray for the truth that shall make men free.

Teach us that liberty is not only to be loved but also to be lived.

Liberty is too precious a thing to be buried in books. It cost too much to be hoarded.

Make us to see that our liberty is not the right to do as we please but the opportunity to please to do what is right.

So may America, through Thy servants, the Members of this body, do what is right, that Thy blessing can rest upon their labours and give them good conscience. Through Jesus Christ our Lord. Amen.

THURSDAY, MARCH 20, 1947

"... Teach us economy in speech ..."

A long, windy debate was going on over the budget. The Senate wished to cut the budget by $4.5 billion. Many sharp words were being spoken. Finally at the suggestion of Senator Knowland (California), it was decided to reduce the national debt rather than taxes.

O Thou who hast the words of eternal life, help us to cultivate proper speech. Surrounded as we are in this city with noble inscriptions of the plain, stirring words of wise men, may we say what we mean and mean what we say. And may it be worth saying. Teach us economy in speech that neither wounds nor offends, that affords light without generating heat. Bridle our tongues lest they stampede us into utterances of which, later, we shall be ashamed. This we ask in Jesus' name. Amen.

FRIDAY, MARCH 21, 1947

"... Help us to stand up for the inalienable rights of mankind and the principles of democratic government ..."

Britain, sapped by the war, was no longer economically able to continue to be the world champion of democratic principles. Greece and Turkey needed to be defended against communist encroachment. The question was: would the

United States now take over this world leadership? Because of the leadership of Senator Vandenberg and Secretary of State Marshall we did accept that leadership.

O Lord our God, in the midst of the troubles that surround us, when compromises come home to roost and expediencies return to plague us, keep us from adding to the mistakes of the past.

Save us from accepting a little of what we know to be wrong in order to get a little of what we imagine to be right.

Help us to stand up for the inalienable rights of mankind and the principles of democratic government consistently and with courage, knowing that Thy power and Thy blessing will be upon us only when we are in the right. May we so speak, and vote, and live, as to merit Thy blessing. Through Jesus Christ our Lord. Amen.

MONDAY, MARCH 24, 1947

". . . the blatant voices of aggressive pressure groups . . ."

Seeing Capitol Hill at close range, Peter Marshall was appalled at the number and persistency of minority pressure groups. He sympathised with the Senators in the dilemma into which this constantly plunged them.

Lord God of hosts, Thou who art concerned about two billions of Thy creatures all over the earth, and yet who art concerned about each of us here as if we were an only child, Thou dost understand how hard it is for these Thy servants to keep in mind the millions of their fellow citizens for whom they must legislate.

Thou knowest the clamour of voices in their ears, the constant tugging at their sleeves, forever trying to influence them; the small voices of the little men without money or names; the blatant voices of aggressive pressure groups; the big voices of selfish men and those working for personal gain; even the whispering inner voices of personal ambition, those insinuating voices holding out the lure of unmerited reward.

Amid all the din of voices, give these Thy servants the willingness to take time to listen to Thy voice, knowing that if they follow the still small voice within, all Thy people will be served fairly and all groups will get what they deserve. For Jesus' sake. Amen.

TUESDAY, MARCH 25, 1947

Our Father in heaven, as we pray for Thy guidance and help, we know that Thou dost not intend prayer to be a substitute for work.

We know that we are expected to do our part, for Thou hast made us, not puppets, but persons with minds to think and wills to resolve. Make us willing to think, and think hard, clearly, and honestly, guided by Thy voice within us, and in accordance with the light Thou hast given us.

May we never fail to do the very best we can. Help us to pray in the knowledge that it all depends on Thee. Help us then to work as if it all depended on us, that together we may do that which is well pleasing in Thy sight. For Jesus' sake. Amen.

WEDNESDAY. MARCH 26, 1947

In the name of Jesus Christ, who was never in a hurry, we pray, O God, that Thou wilt slow us down, for we know that we live too fast. If we are to burn ourselves out, may it be in causes worth dying for.

With all of eternity before us, make us take time to live —time to get acquainted with Thee, time to enjoy Thy blessings, and time to know each other. Deliver us from wasting time and teach us how to use it wisely and well. We ask these things in the lovely name of Jesus. Amen.

THURSDAY, MARCH 27, 1947

"... our great need of Thy guidance ..."

The question of whether to end sugar rationing was being debated. The Senators were harried by thousands of letters from housewives begging that control not be continued.

On this day one of the Senators approached Peter at

*the close of his prayer. "I've been listening pretty closely
to your prayers," he said. "You seem to think a man can
get specific guidance from God about his work. Tell me
now, do you really think God could tell someone like me
how to vote on the Sugar Bill?"*

*Peter felt that this was sincere seeking, and it heartened
him to know that his prayers were pointing the men to the
real source of the wisdom they constantly needed.*

Our Father, we stand to join our hearts in prayer in our
acknowledgment of our great need of Thy guidance. We
know that by ourselves we are not sufficient for these days
or for problems beyond the measure of our best wisdom.

We are finding out that government of the people by the
people is not good enough. We pray for government of
the people by God.

As this Nation was founded under God, so we confess that
our freedom, too, must be under God. Then, and only
then, shall we achieve the peace we seek and the righteousness which alone exalteth a nation.

Hear our prayer, O God, and grant unto the Members
of this body Thy guidance, we humbly beseech Thee in
Jesus' name. Amen.

FRIDAY, MARCH 28, 1947

". . . Thy solutions to the questions that perplex
us . . ."

*For ten weeks the Senate had been debating the appointment
of David E. Lilienthal as a member of the Atomic Energy
Commission.*

*This procrastination was finally ended by a masterly speech
by Arthur Vandenberg, President pro tem of the Senate.*

*Though Peter usually left immediately after his prayer, on
those occasions when Vandenberg turned the Chair over to
someone else and took the floor, Peter always stayed to hear
him speak.*

Lord Jesus, who didst promise that by faith Thy disciples
might remove mountains, increase our faith till we no
longer are awed by difficulties and frightened by problems.
Hold us by Thy mighty hand until doubts shall cease and

93

we begin to believe. Then shall we find all things possible, even Thy solutions to the questions that perplex us. For this we do pray. Amen.

MONDAY, MARCH 31, 1947

Our Father, as we seek Thy blessing, remind us that we cannot deceive ourselves.

We dare not devise our own plans and draft our own schemes and then have the nerve to ask Thee to bless them, for we know that there are some things Thou wilt not and cannot bless.

And unless Thy blessing accompanies what we do here, we waste our time. So guide us in what we propose, so that Thou canst bless us in what we produce. Through Jesus Christ our Lord. Amen.

TUESDAY, APRIL 1, 1947

When we are honestly perplexed and have to do something, and are not sure what to do, we need Thy help, O God. In our choices let us not ask, "Will it work?" but rather, "Is it right?" In this prayer we reach up to Thee. May we find that Thou art reaching down to us, and may we believe that when we are willing to listen, Thou wilt speak. We wait upon Thee, O God. Through Jesus Christ our Lord. Amen.

WEDNESDAY, APRIL 2, 1947

O God, who didst love us all so much that Thou didst send us Jesus Christ for the illumination of our darkness and the salvation of our souls, give us wisdom to profit by the words He spoke, faith to accept the salvation He offers, and grace to follow in His steps.

As Christ said: "When ye stand praying, forgive, if ye have aught against any." O God, give us grace now so to do.

As Christ said: "It is more blessed to give than to receive." O God, give us grace today to think not of what we can get but of what we can give.

As Christ said: "Judge not, that ye be not judged." O God, give us grace this day first to cast the beam out of our own eyes before we regard the mote that is in our brothers' eyes. And when we find it hard to be humble, hard to forgive, O Lord, remind us how much harder it was to hang on the Cross. Amen.

THURSDAY, APRIL 3, 1947

On the night of April 2 the Senate was in Session until midnight.[1] There had been a steady four hours of debate, climaxing ten weeks of discussion over the appointment of David E. Lilienthal as chairman of the Atomic Energy Commission.

The Senators were exhausted; Senatorial tempers were raw. At almost midnight, Senator Morse wanted the floor; Senator Wherry moved a recess and refused to yield the floor to Morse. The motion to recess carried. Immediately afterwards there were a few sharp words between Wherry and Morse.

The Washington papers the next morning exaggerated the incident into a near fist fight. Peter had not seen the papers and knew nothing of the incident when he wrote or delivered the prayer which follows.

But the prayer spoke to Senator Wherry's heart. He thought his minister was praying right at him. After the prayer, he followed Peter into the corridor. "Parson," he said, "I guess you know God pretty well. You know the Catholics believe in having a father-confessor. Will you be mine? I'm awfully sorry for what happened last night . . ."

This incident gave Peter a great lift. Obviously, the Spirit of God was at work in the United States Senate.

Gracious Father, we, Thy children, so often confused, live at cross-purposes in our central aims, and hence we are at cross-purposes with each other. Take us by the hand and help us to see things from Thy viewpoint, that we may see them as they really are. We come to choices and decisions with a prayer upon our lips, for our wisdom fails us. Give us Thine, that we may do Thy will. In Jesus' name. Amen.

[1] See pages 250 to 251 of *A Man Called Peter.*

MONDAY, APRIL 7, 1947

We know, our Father, that there is a time to speak and a time to keep silence. Help us to tell the one from the other. When we should speak, give us the courage of our convictions. When we should keep silence, restrain us from speaking, lest, in our desire to appear wise, we give ourselves away.

Teach us the sacraments of silence that we may use them to know ourselves and, above us, to know Thee. Then shall we be wise. Through Jesus Christ our Lord. Amen.

TUESDAY, APRIL 8, 1947

Almighty and eternal God, Thou who alone knowest what lies before us this day, grant that in every hour of it we may stay close to Thee. Let us today embark on no undertaking that is not in line with Thy will for us here, for our country and our world.

Bestow Thy grace upon the Presiding Officer, the Members, and the servants of this body. Illumine our minds and direct our thinking, that our thoughts and our actions may merit Thy blessing. For our Lord Christ's sake. Amen.

WEDNESDAY, APRIL 9, 1947

Our fathers' God, to Thee, who art the author of our liberty, and under whom we have our freedom, we make our prayer.

Make us ever mindful of the price that was paid to obtain that freedom and the cost that must be met to keep it. Help us in this Nation so to live it that other men shall desire and seek after it. Believing in it, give us the backbone to stand up for it. Loving it, may we be willing to defend it. In the strong name of Him who said, "If ye continue in My word, ye shall know the truth, and the truth shall make you free." Amen.

THURSDAY, APRIL 10, 1947

Our Father in heaven, we give Thee thanks for good weather and the lovely promises of spring. We thank Thee for good health, good friends, and all the things we so often take for granted.

We thank Thee for the keen challenges of this hour, for work to do that demands the best we have and still finds us inadequate.

Then may we seek Thy help, knowing that in partnership with Thee, in applying Thy will to our problems, there shall be no dull moments and no problems beyond solution. God bless us all and help us to be right and to do right. Through Jesus Christ our Lord. Amen.

FRIDAY, APRIL 11, 1947

We come in prayer to Thee, Lord Jesus, who never had to take back anything spoken, to correct anything said, or to apologise for any statement. Wilt Thou have pity upon our frailties and deliver us from pitying ourselves.

Bless the Members of this body as they think together and work together in this Chamber, in committee rooms, and in their offices. Help them to stand up under the strains and the tensions of problems and decisions, of meetings and conferences, and the endless demands made upon them. Teach them how to relax and to take time to turn to Thee for guidance and for grace, and thus discover the secret of power. In Thy name we ask it. Amen.

WEDNESDAY, APRIL 16, 1947

O Lord our God, in the face of life's mysteries and its vast imponderables, give us faith to believe that Thou makest all things to work together for good to them that love Thee.

Strengthen our conviction that Thy hand is upon us, to lead us and to use us in working out Thy purposes in the world. Even though we may not see the distant scene, let us be willing to take one step at a time and trust Thee for the rest. Through Jesus Christ. Amen.

O God, our Father, in whom is our trust, Thou alone dost know the end from the beginning, and we, Thy children, must needs walk by faith.

We are anxious about the consequences of what we do. May that concern restrain us in our private lives as it does in our public duty.

In our troubled minds there is confusion and honest perplexity. But we know there is no confusion with Thee. Wilt Thou guide us, that we may do what is right; and if we suffer for it, we shall be blessed. This we ask in Christ's name, who was crucified, having done nothing amiss. Amen.

FRIDAY, APRIL 18, 1947

Our Father, we yearn for a better understanding of spiritual things that we may know surely what Thy will is for us and for our Nation. Give to us clear vision that we may know where to stand and what to stand for—because " unless we stand for something, we shall fall for anything."

Remind us, O God, that Thou hast not resigned. Harassed and troubled by the difficulties, and uncertainties of the hour, we rest our minds on Thee, who dost not change. May it ever be in our minds as upon our coins that in God we trust. For Jesus' sake. Amen.

MONDAY, APRIL 21, 1947

Lord Jesus, help us to see clearly that the pace at which we are living these days shuts Thee out of our minds and hearts, and leaves us, even with good intentions, to wander in the misty land of half-truth and compromise.

Deliver us, O God, from the God-helps-those-who-help-themselves philosophy, which is really a cloak for sheer unbelief in Thy ability and willingness to take care of us and our affairs.

Give to us a passion for that which is in principle excellent rather than in politics expedient, for that which is morally right rather than socially correct. These things we ask in Jesus' name. Amen.

The Senators were hurried and under constant time pressure. Their chaplain understood the problem of busy men making "time their servant and not their master."

Lord Jesus, who didst fill three short years with the revelation of all eternity, in life, precept, and promise, that we have not yet learned and can never forget, help us to make every minute count, making time our servant and not our master. Thou didst never ask for time to prepare Thine answers but always had the word of Truth for every occasion. Reveal to us now Thy word for today. Amen.

"... when we say 'No' to Thee, we are denying our own best interest. ..."

Increased exports to meet the economic need in Europe might well send prices up in the United States. The question was whether this danger was worse than the collapse of the rest of the world. In general the Senate did proceed to act in a responsible manner concerning the needs of the world.

Our Father, help us to understand that when we try to live without Thee, we are unable to live with ourselves, and when we say "No" to Thee, we are denying our own best interest. Whatever other rewards or punishments Thou hast ordained, we are finding out that we cannot do wrong and feel right, for there is a law within Thy universe that acts around us and in us.

Give to each of us, we pray, that intelligent self-interest that shall persuade us to do Thy will. Teach us that obeying Thee and Thy will is a forced option—like eating. We do not have to eat, but if we do not, we cannot live. We are not forced to obey Thee, but if we do not, we hurt ourselves. Convict us of the folly of walking against Thy lights that we may live, longer and better. By the grace and mercy of Jesus Christ our Lord. Amen.

" . . . May we confess our part in creating our dilemmas. . . ."

Sometimes the Congress made shortsighted decisions. It was little wonder! Overworked Senators were having to make dozens of decisions for conquered and liberated countries.

To cite one example, the United States and her Allies were busy destroying Germany's capacity to manufacture fertilizers by destroying her nitrogen and phosphoric acid plants. This was meant to circumvent any conversion to future munitions manufacture, but it wasn't helping agriculture in starving Europe. A dilemma indeed!

Our Father, we in this place are weighed down by the problems of our Nation and of our world. Convict us of our share of personal responsibility for the situation in which we find ourselves. May we confess our part in creating our dilemmas, lest we feel no obligation to solve them.

Help us to quit waiting for the other fellow to change his attitude and his ways, lest we never give Thee the chance for which Thou hast been waiting, to change us. This we ask in the lovely name of Him who came to change us all, even Jesus Christ our Lord. Amen.

Our Father which art in heaven, we pray for all the people of our country, that they may learn to appreciate more the goodly heritage that is ours.

We need to learn, in these challenging days, that to every right there is attached a duty and to every privilege an obligation. We believe that, in the eternal order of things, Thou hast so ordained it, and what Thou hast joined together, let us not try to put asunder.

Teach us what freedom is. May we all learn the lesson that it is not the right to do as we please but the opportunity to please to do what is right.

Above all, may we discover that wherever the Spirit of the

Lord is, there is freedom. May we have that freedom now, in His presence here, to lead us and to help us keep this Nation free. This we ask in Jesus' name. Amen.

MONDAY, APRIL 28, 1947

We unite our hearts, O God, in this prayer that Thou wilt teach us how to trust in Thee as a Heavenly Father who loves us and who is concerned about what we do and what we are.

Forgive us that there are times when we find it hard, when it ought to be easy. It is not that we have no faith, but that we seem so reluctant to put our faith in Thee.

Men have proved to be untrustworthy, yet we trust each other. Banks have failed, still we write our cheques. Depressions have upset our economy, still we carry on business in faith. Blizzards have made the winter drear, yet with the coming of spring we plant our seeds. Hurricanes have screamed across the land, yet we build our windmills.

Give to us the faith to put our trust in Thee who dost hold in the hollow of Thy hand all things living. May we learn, before we blunder, that Thou art willing to lead us, to show us what to do, and that it is possible for us to know Thy will and to be partners with Thee in doing what is right. This we ask in the name of Christ, who never made a mistake. Amen.

TUESDAY, APRIL 29, 1947

Give us open eyes, our Father, to see the beauty all around us and to see it in Thy handiwork. Let all lovely things fill us with gladness and let them lift up our hearts in true worship.

Give us this day, O Lord, a strong and vivid sense that Thou art by our side. By Thy grace, let us go nowhere this day where Thou canst not come nor court any companionship that would rob us of Thine. Through Jesus Christ our Lord. Amen.

" . . . the little progress of the conference just concluded across the seas . . ."

The Moscow Conference was over. The United States and the U.S.S.R. had been at odds over every major question. We were unwilling to have puppet states made of Germany and Austria.

Our Father in heaven, who dost love the whole world, save us from despair and fear as we ponder the little progress of the conference just concluded across the seas. Help us to see that there is gain in our statement of faith while others voice their fears, and that nothing is lost when our convictions and principles are expressed boldly and honestly in the midst of intrigue and suspicion.

Keep us ever resolute in striving for the things for which so many of our men gave their lives in battle. Let us not throw away their sacrifice.

Since we seek unity and harmony in the world and in our own land, help us to achieve it in this place. If we, Thy servants, who pray together, who speak the same language, who share the same basic ideals, cannot work as a team, what hope have we that the leaders of other nations, with different languages, who do not pray together, whose ideals are so different, can achieve agreement?

Help us, a hundred men, to find the secret of agreement, that we may show it to our own Nation and lead it into teamwork between management and labour, between every group and faction, that our Nation may be one.

As we express our own ideas and listen to the ideas of those who differ with us, may we be humble enough to think about the third idea—Thine—and be persuaded by Thy Holy Spirit to embrace it, and thus discover the secret of harmony. In the name of Jesus Christ, who was always right. Amen.

THURSDAY, MAY 1, 1947

The prayer which follows is a good example of Dr Marshall's down-to-earth approach.

Our Father, we would not weary Thee in always asking for something. This morning we would pray that Thou wouldst take something from us. Take out of our hearts any bitterness that lies there, any resentment that curdles and corrodes our peace.

Take away the stubborn pride that keeps us from apology and confessing fault and makes us unwilling to open our hearts to one another. For if our hearts are closed to our colleagues, they are not open to Thee. We ask Thy mercy in Jesus' name. Amen.

FRIDAY, MAY 2, 1947

O Lord, Thou dost know the secrets that will remake Thy world, for Thou art the way. Help us to see that the forces that threaten the freedoms for which we fought cannot be argued down, nor can they be shot down. They must be lived down. Give to the leaders of our Nation the inspired ideas that shall lead this country into making the American dream come true. Through Jesus Christ our Lord. Amen.

MONDAY, MAY 5, 1947

Most gracious God, facing the activities and the opportunities of another week, may we be eager and not reluctant. Keep us ever alert to the need for change and open as channels for divine power. Help us to keep keen the edges of our minds, to keep our thinking straight and true.

Give us the will to keep our passions in control and the common sense to keep our bodies fit and healthy, that we may be able to do what Thou hast called us to do. Through Jesus Christ our Lord. Amen.

Forgive us, O God, that in this land so richly blessed by Thee, we, Thy people, have been wasteful. We have wasted the measures of the earth, stolen the virtues of the soil, in failing to restore after we had received.

But we have been wasteful of ourselves. We have wasted our strength in enterprises not inspired of Thee. We have wasted our talents in unworthy causes, wasted our love in loving the unlovely. We have wasted our money for that which satisfieth not. We have wasted our time in activities that profited nothing.

Forgive us all wherein we have been prodigal, and like the young son, help us to come to ourselves that we may come to Thee to be forgiven and restored. This we ask in Jesus' name. Amen.

WEDNESDAY, MAY 7, 1947

" . . . the pressures that drive us and the tensions that break us down . . ."

Two days earlier, Representative Charles Gerlach (Pennsylvania), aged fifty-one, had died of a heart attack. Peter was acutely aware of the tension under which the Representatives and Senators worked. . . .

O God, our Father, who has given us life and made our earth so fair, reveal to us this day Thy heart of infinite tenderness yearning for our love.

Make us to feel Thy Spirit brooding over us, longing to help us in our decisions, to save us from the pressures that drive us and the tensions that break us down.

How strange it is, O Lover of our souls, that Thou who art love, who dost give love to hungry human hearts, shouldst Thyself be the great unloved. Give us love to love Thee for Thy love, and to love Him who first loved us and gave Himself for us. Loving Thee, we shall love one another, and loving one another, we shall do Thy will, and doing Thy will, we shall always do right. We make our prayer in the lovely name of Jesus. Amen.

Before going into the Vice-President's office to meet Senator Vandenberg, Peter often had an informal chat with Mr John D. Rhodes in the office of the Reporters of Senate Debate.

On this particular day he read his prayer to Mr Rhodes. "I want your opinion about it," he said. Mr Rhodes was mildly shocked. "I don't know what to say, Peter. It's pretty daring—"

But the prayer was used just as it stood. The Associated Press picked it up, and it subsequently received very wide publicity.

We open our hearts unto Thee, our Father, and pray that Thy spirit may indwell each one of us and give us poise and power. We believe in Thee, O God. Give us the faith to believe what Thou hast said. We trust in Thee, O God. Give us the faith to trust Thee for guidance in the decisions we have to make.

Help us to do our very best this day and be content with today's troubles, so that we shall not borrow the troubles of tomorrow. Save us from the sin of worrying, lest stomach ulcers be the badge of our lack of faith. Amen.

In this, the day that the Lord hath made, help us, O God, to appreciate its beauty and to use aright its opportunities.

Deliver us, we pray Thee, from the tyranny of trifles. May we give our best thought and attention to what is important, that we may accomplish something worthwhile. Teach us how to listen to the prompting of Thy Spirit, and thus save us from floundering in indecision that wastes time, subtracts from our peace, divides our efficiency, and multiplies our troubles. In the name of Christ Jesus our Lord. Amen.

" . . . the will to work together as a team for the welfare of all our people. . . ."

Discussion of the Taft-Hartley Bill was raging. Many thought it was needlessly vengeful to labour. Teamwork was sorely needed.

Our Father, give us the faith to believe that the words now spoken, and the yearnings of the hearts now open before Thee, are heard and understood in Thy presence.

We, the Members and officers and servants of this body, unite our petitions for Thy blessing, Thy guidance, and Thy help, that we faithfully may do what is best for the people and what is right in Thy sight, O God. Give to these, Thy servants, the representatives of the people in different parts of our land, the will to work together as a team for the welfare of all our people.

Give them courage to withstand the pressure of the selfish, and give to the people the vision to see that sacrifice must be shared by all, that there is no substitute for hard work and no joy in unmerited reward.

May we fear nothing, save that, knowing what is right, we fail to do it. So help us God, in Jesus' name. Amen.

Forbid it, Lord, that "we should walk through Thy beautiful world with unseeing eyes." Forgive us, our Father, for taking our good things for granted, so that we are in danger of losing the fine art of appreciation. With such dire need in every other part of the world, make us so grateful for the bounties we enjoy that we shall try, by Thy help, to deserve them more.

Where we are wrong, make us willing to change, and where we are right, make us easy to live with. For Jesus' sake. Amen.

Lord Jesus, when we get sick of ourselves, ashamed of our littleness, our selfishness, and the petty things that irritate us, then let it be the beginning of spiritual health by making us willing to have Thee create in us clean hearts and renew right spirits within us.

Hold us steady lest we lose our poise. Blunt our speech lest by cutting words and careless deeds we hurt our colleagues and the cause for which we speak.

Where we differ in approaches to a problem, may we ever be open to consider another and a better way, guided not by whether it be popular, or expedient, or practical, but always whether it be right. Hear our prayer, O Lord, and help us, through Jesus Christ. Amen.

THURSDAY, MAY 22, 1947

God of our fathers, give unto us, Thy servants, a true appreciation of our heritage, of great men and great deeds in the past, but let us not be intimidated by feelings of our own inadequacy for this troubled hour.

Remind us that the God they worshipped and by whose help they laid the foundations of our Nation, is still able to help us uphold what they bequeathed and to give it new meanings.

Remind us that we are not called to fill the places of those who have gone, but to fill our own places, to do the work Thou hast laid before us, to do the right as Thou hast given us to see the right, always to do the very best we can, and to leave the rest to Thee. Amen.

FRIDAY, MAY 23, 1947

O Lord our God, shed the light of Thy Holy Spirit within the minds and hearts of Thy servants in this place of responsibility and decision, that all who sincerely seek the truth may find it, and finding it may follow it, whatever the cost, knowing that it is the truth that makes men free.

When we have the truth, let us not hit each other over

the head with it, but rather use it as a lamp to lighten dark places, in order that we may see where we are going. This we ask in the name of Jesus Christ our Lord. Amen.

MONDAY, MAY 26, 1947

We thank Thee, our Father in heaven, for this sacred moment when our hearts may be united in prayer, and when forgetting all else save our need of Thy guidance and help, we may reach up to Thee as Thou art reaching down to us.

Let not the beauty of this day, or the glow of good health, or the present prosperity of our undertakings deceive us into a false reliance upon our own strength. Thou hast given us every good thing. Thou hast given us life itself with whatever talents we possess and the time and the opportunity to use them. May we use them wisely, lest they be curtailed or taken away.

Deliver us from the error of asking and expecting Thy blessing and Thy guidance in our public lives while closing the doors to Thee in our private living. Thou knowest what we are wherever we are. Help us to be the best we can be. We ask in the name of Jesus Christ our Lord. Amen.

WEDNESDAY, MAY 28, 1947

If Thou, O Lord, shouldst mark iniquities, who among us could stand unafraid before Thee? For there is so much bad in the best of us, and so much good in the worst of us, that we dare not criticise each other. But Thou canst reprove us all.

Ere we begin our duties, cleanse Thou our minds and hearts. What no proper shame kept us from committing, let no false shame keep us from confessing. In this moment may we find grace to seek Thy pardon and find the joy of the Gospel of making a new beginning. In the power of Christ our Lord and Master. Amen.

"The long week-end" was Memorial Day week-end, which was marked by a series of tragic air accidents. In Japan an Army C-54 rammed into a mountain; in Iceland a DC-3 crashed; at LaGuardia Field, New York a DC-4 crashed; before June 2 was over, another DC-4 fell into a Maryland bog. Total casualties—160.

Once again, our Father, the long week-end that brings rest and refreshment to so many of our people has brought disaster and sorrow to some, and our Nation is sobered in the reflection that death is in the midst of life. Since we know not at what moment the slender thread may be broken for us, teach us to number our days that we may apply our hearts unto wisdom. And may we be compassionate, remembering the hearts that are sore and our brethren who languish in sorrow and affliction.

Take from us the selfishness that is unwilling to bear the burdens of others while expecting that others shall help us with ours. Make us so disgusted with our big professions and our little deeds, our fine words and our shabby thoughts, our friendly faces and our cold hearts, that we shall pray sincerely this morning for a new spirit and new attitudes. Then shall our prayers mean something, not alone to ourselves but to our Nation. In the name of Jesus Christ our Lord. Amen.

We pray, O God, that Thou wilt fill this sacred minute with meaning, and make it an oasis for the refreshment of our souls, a window-cleaning for our vision, and a re-charging of the batteries of our spirits. Let us have less talking and more thinking, less work and more worship, less pressure and more prayer. For if we are too busy to pray, we are far busier than we have any right to be.

Speak to us, O Lord, and make us listen to Thy broadcasting station that never goes off the air. Through Thy Holy Spirit, who is waiting to lead us into all truth. Amen.

O Lord our God, as we seek Thy guidance this day we do not ask to see the distant scene, knowing that we can take only one step at a time. Make that first step plain to us, that we may see where our duty lies, but give us a push, that we may start in the right direction. Through Jesus Christ our Lord. Amen.

THURSDAY, JUNE 5, 1947

" . . . if it be Thy will that America should assume world leadership . . ."

On this day, the Secretary of State Gen. George C. Marshall gave a speech at Harvard urging an economically integrated Europe. He wanted United States help to be on a Europe-wide, not nation-by-nation basis. This speech was the Nation's introduction to the Marshall Plan for aid to Europe.

Our Heavenly Father, if it be Thy will that America should assume world leadership, as history demands and the hopes of so many nations desire, make us good enough to undertake it.

We consider our resources in money and in men, yet forget the spiritual resources without which we dare not and cannot lead the world.

Forgive us all for our indifference to the means of grace Thou hast appointed. Thy Word, the best-seller of all books, remains among us the great unread, the great unbelieved, the great ignored.

Turn our thoughts again to that Book which alone reveals what man is to believe concerning God and what duty God requires of man.

Thus informed, thus directed, we shall understand the spiritual laws by which alone peace can be secured, and learn what is the righteousness that alone exalteth a nation. For the sake of the world's peace and our own salvation, we pray in the name of Christ, Thy revelation. Amen.

". . . In spite of present difficulties. . . ."

The Communists had just seized Hungary, and the people of the United States were outraged at this violation of the Yalta Agreement.

O God, our Heavenly Father, restore our faith in the ultimate triumph of Thy plan for the world Thou hast made. In spite of present difficulties, our disappointments, and our fears, reassure us that Thou art still in control.

When we become frustrated and give up, remind us that Thou art still holding things together, waiting and working and watching. When we make mistakes, help us to remember that Thou dost not give up on us.

Forbid it, Lord, that we should give up on Thee and forget that all things work together for good to them that love Thee. Through Jesus Christ our Lord. Amen.

MONDAY, JUNE 9, 1947

Forgive us, O God, that we are so anxious in all we say and do, to have the approval of men, forgetting that it is Thy approval that brings us peace of mind and clear conscience. Make us aware of the record Thou art writing —the record that one day will be read by the Judge of all the universe. We need to remember that there is no party in integrity, no politics in goodness. We pray for Thy grace and Thy help to do better and to be better. Through Jesus Christ. Amen.

TUESDAY, JUNE 10, 1947

O Lord of our lives, wilt Thou teach us true discrimination, that we may be able to discern the difference between faith and fatalism, between activity and accomplishment, between humility and an inferiority complex, between a passing salute to God and a real prayer that seeks to find out God's will?

We can stand criticism. We can stand a certain amount of

pressure. But we cannot stand, O God, the necessity of making grave decisions with nothing but our own poor human wisdom. Our heads are not enough and our hearts fail us.

Cabbages have heads, but they have no souls. We, who are created in the image of God, are restless and unhappy until we know that we are doing Thy will by Thy help. This is what we pray for, through Jesus Christ our Lord. Amen.

WEDNESDAY, JUNE 11, 1947

Our Father in heaven, as we unite in prayer for Thy blessings upon the Members of this body, we know that Thou art lovingly concerned about the way we live and how we wear ourselves out, taking less care of ourselves than we do of our cars.

Bless Thy Servants, the Senators, with good health, and the good sense to preserve it. Bless the members of their families. May they commit them all to Thy care, that no leaden anxiety shall keep any man from doing his best work.

We feel that we have to do so many things that we would rather not do, as we plead that we have no time to do some things we know very well we should do. Help us to make wise choices and proper use of our time. We wait upon Thee for the continual answer to our prayers. In the name of Christ, Thy Son. Amen.

FRIDAY, JUNE 13, 1947

God of our fathers, in whose name this Republic was born, we pray that by Thy help we may be worthy to receive Thy blessings upon our labours.

In the troubled and uneasy travail before the birth of lasting peace, when men have made deceit a habit, lying an art, and cruelty a science, help us to show the moral superiority of the way of life we cherish. Here may men see truth upheld, honesty loved, and kindness practised.

In our dealings with each other, may we be gentle, understanding, and kind, with our tempers under control.

In our dealings with other nations, may we be firm without obstinacy, generous without extravagance, and right without compromise. We do not pray that other nations may love us, but that they may know that we stand for what is right, unafraid, with the courage of our convictions.

May our private lives and our public actions be consistent with our prayers. Through Jesus Christ our Lord. Amen.

MONDAY, JUNE 16, 1947

We confess, our Father, that we know in our hearts how much we need Thee, yet our swelled heads and our stubborn wills keep us trying to do without Thee.

Forgive us for making so many mountains out of molehills and for exaggerating both our own importance and the problems that confront us.

Make us willing to let Thee show us what a difference Thou couldst make in our work, increasing our success and diminishing our failures. Give us the faith to believe that if we give Thee a hearing Thou wilt give us the answers we cannot find by ourselves. In Jesus' name. Amen.

TUESDAY, JUNE 17, 1947

Thou must be grieved, O Lord, that, after nineteen hundred years, mankind never seems to learn how to live by faith, and still prefers worry to trust in God. We know what worry does to us, yet are all too reluctant to discover what faith could do.

Since we strain at gnats and swallow camels, give us a new standard of values and the ability to know a trifle when we see it and to deal with it as such. Let us not waste the time Thou hast given us. So help us, God. Amen.

WEDNESDAY, JUNE 18, 1947

Once again, our Father, we come to Thee in prayer, on the same terms, because of our need of Thy help, and our faith that Thou dost govern in the affairs of men and wilt hear our prayer in the name of Christ, Thy Son.

Thou hast given us the inner voice of conscience, and Thy

113

Holy Spirit enables us to distinguish good from evil. But where we are to choose between two courses when both are good and commendable, then we need the crystal clarity of Thy guidance, that we may see one to be better than the other. Help us, O God, at the point of our uncertainty, for there is no uncertainty with Thee. Thou hast a plan. We would clasp Thy hand. That shall be to us "better than light and safer than a known way." Through Jesus Christ our Lord. Amen.

THURSDAY, JUNE 19, 1947

The Senate pageboys like the "straight-shooting" of a prayer like the one which follows—and told Peter so.

O God, our Father, while we pride ourselves that we learn something every day, we seem to make little progress in spiritual things.

Nowhere is our ignorance more tragic. So long have we been riding on the balloon tyres of conceit, for our own good we may have to be deflated, that on the rims of humility we may discover the spiritual laws that govern our growth in grace.

If our pride has to be punctured, Lord, make it soon, before we gain too much speed. For the salvation of our souls and the good of our country. In Jesus' name. Amen.

MONDAY, JUNE 23, 1947

We thank Thee, O Lord, that this land is still governed by the people's representatives. Let democratic processes be seen at their best in this time of testing.

As these chosen men discharge their duties, guide them, O God, in the decisions they must make today. Give them the grace of humility, and shed now Thy guiding light into every mind. Break down every will that is stubbornly set against Thine or that has ignored Thee.

May what is done be so clearly right that it needs no incendiary justification. Soothe our still smouldering hearts and minds with the spirit of forgiveness. Let us be swayed not by emotion or ambition but by calm conviction. This we ask in Jesus' name. Amen.

Our Father, when we become satisfied with ourselves, hold ever before us Thy demands for perfection.

Lest we become content with a good batting average, let us see the absolutes of honesty, of love, and of obedience to Thy will Thou dost require of us. Seeing them, may we strive after them by Thy help. Through Jesus Christ our Lord. Amen.

Our Father, we are beginning to understand at last that the things that are wrong with our world are the sum total of all the things that are wrong with us as individuals. Thou hast made us after Thine image, and our hearts can find no rest until they rest in Thee.

We are too Christian really to enjoy sinning and too fond of sinning really to enjoy Christianity. Most of us know perfectly well what we ought to do; our trouble is that we do not want to do it. Thy help is our only hope. Make us want to do what is right, and give us the ability to do it. In the name of Christ our Lord. Amen.

Teach us, O Lord, the disciplines of patience, for we find that to wait is often harder than to work.

When we wait upon Thee, we shall not be ashamed, but shall renew our strength.

May we be willing to stop our feverish activities and listen to what Thou hast to say, that our prayers shall not be the sending of night letters, but conversations with God. This we ask in Jesus' name. Amen.

Lord Jesus, we know of no better way to begin the work of another week than by rededicating our lives to Thee, resolving to trust Thee and to obey Thee, and to do our very best to serve by serving our fellow men.

In these days that call for understanding, for mercy, for the salvation of men's souls and the healing of their bodies, may we have Thy Spirit that we may work to that end, for Thou art the Saviour of the world, and we have no hope apart from Thee. Hear our prayer for Thy mercy's sake. Amen.

TUESDAY, JULY 1, 1947

Teach us, our Father, how to look at the things we see, and to look at them without bias or prejudice. We may not know how much of our troubles are caused by refusing to look at the facts or by viewing them so differently.

We are all too familiar with " dirty looks," " scornful looks," " unbelieving looks," " black looks." Give to us discerning and understanding looks. With the truth waiting to be looked at, discovered, and applied, forgive us when we refuse to look at it or to welcome it.

If Thou wilt help us to cast the mote of prejudice and pride out of our eyes, then shall we see clearly. We pray for good sight and good sense, in the name of Jesus Christ. Amen.

WEDNESDAY, JULY 2, 1947

Lord of our lives, we pray that Thou wilt fill with new meanings this sacred moment of prayer. Help us to feel and to believe that we are talking with God. In this interlude of intercession, may we forget all else save our deep need of Thy guidance and Thy help.

In our hearts are fears and frustrations, and we cannot view the future of our world without misgivings. If there is a way for this God-believing Nation to live at peace with nations that deny Thee, Thou wilt have to reveal it to us, for we have not found it yet.

The disappointments and indecisions in our own lives teach us that we, ourselves, are not in tune with Thy will for us. God help us, and save us, and tell us what to do.

May the Great Physician minister to our brethren in

sickness, and the sympathising Jesus be near to those in trouble, and the Holy Spirit be in our hearts and minds this day, we ask in Jesus' name. Amen.

THURSDAY, JULY 3, 1947

God of our fathers, whose Almighty hand hath made and preserved our Nation, grant that our people may understand what it is they celebrate tomorrow.

May they remember how bitterly our freedom was won, the down payment that was made for it, the instalments that have been made since this Republic was born, and the price that must yet be paid for our liberty.

May freedom be seen not as the right to do as we please but as the opportunity to please to do what is right.

May it ever be understood that our liberty is under God and can be found nowhere else.

May our faith be something that is not merely stamped upon our coins, but expressed in our lives.

Let us, as a nation, not be afraid of standing alone for the rights of men, since we were born that way, as the only nation on earth that came into being " for the glory of God and the advancement of the Christian faith."

We know that we shall be true to the Pilgrim dream when we are true to the God they worshipped.

To the extent that America honours Thee, wilt Thou bless America, and keep her true as Thou hast kept her free, and make her good as Thou hast made her rich. Amen.

MONDAY, NOVEMBER 17, 1947

" . . . hunger that knows no politics and want that will not wait. . . ."   " . . . what Thy plan is. . . ."

Congress was called back into session by President Truman, who asked for sweeping peacetime controls over our economy, to head off rising inflation.

Western Europe was running a deficit of $5 billion a year in fuel, grain, oils, and basic commodities. Secretary of State Marshall warned the Nation that a crisis was imminent. If European civilization collapsed, the receiver would be Russia.

It was characteristic of Peter Marshall that, while others on Capitol Hill were, during this period, talking about the Truman Plan, the Marshall Plan, the European Recovery Plan, he was unabashedly talking about God's plan.

O God, our Father, we pray for Thy wisdom and Thy guidance for the Members of this body as they meet in this troubled hour to consider what this Nation should do about hunger that knows no politics and want that will not wait.

We cannot escape history: that we have found out. May we also discover that we cannot evade responsibility. By Thy Holy Spirit awaken the conscience of America, that our people may be willing to put humanity first.

Give to our leaders the highest motives and the courage to propose that which will be worthy of Thy blessing, lest we do the right things for the wrong reasons.

Help our Senators to see what Thy plan is, in the name of Jesus Christ, who, being rich, for our sakes became poor. Amen.

MONDAY, NOVEMBER 24, 1947

God of our fathers and our God, give us the faith to believe in the ultimate triumph of righteousness, no matter how dark and uncertain are the skies of today.

We pray for the bifocals of faith—that see the despair and the need of the hour but also see, further on, the patience of our God working out His plan in the world He has made.

So help Thy servants to interpret for our time the meaning of the motto inscribed on our coins.

Make our faith honest by helping us this day to do one thing because Thou hast said, "Do it," or to abstain because Thou hast said, "Thou shalt not".

How can we say we believe in Thee, or even want to believe in Thee, when we do not anything Thou dost tell us?

May our faith be seen in our works. Through Jesus Christ our Lord. Amen.

O Lord, keep strong our faith in the efficacy of prayer as we unite our petitions in this sacred moment.

We have asked for Thy guidance in difficult decisions many times, yet it has not always come when we thought it should come. Many of the situations and relationships which we have asked Thee to change have remained the same.

Forgive us for thinking, therefore, that Thou art unwilling to help us in our dilemmas, or that there is nothing Thou canst do.

Remind us, our Father, that when we plug in an electric iron and it fails to work, we do not conclude that electricity has lost its power, nor do we plead with the iron. We look at once to the wiring to find what has broken or blocked connection with the source of power.

May we do the same with ourselves, that Thou mayest work through us to do Thy will. This we ask in Jesus' name. Amen.

WEDNESDAY, NOVEMBER 26, 1947

"... there exists ... an indescribable union ... between duty and advantage. ..."

A Thanksgiving Day Prayer. After seven months of debate, the world's greatest trading nations, led by the United States, took a long step toward unclogging the world's trade channels. Tariffs were much reduced. We pegged tariff rates to the then-present level on 20 per cent of dutiable imports, cut from 25 per cent to 50 per cent on the rest.

The Geneva conference also worked out the basic principle that all negotiators would have to benefit from any tariff cuts granted.

Peter Marshall saw all this as heartening progress toward " One World"—the Kingdom of God on earth.

Our Father in heaven, if ever we had cause to offer unto Thee our fervent thanks, surely it is now, on the eve of our Thanksgiving Day, when we, the people of this Nation, are comfortable, well-fed, well-clad, and blessed with good things beyond our deserving. May gratitude, the rarest of all virtues, be the spirit of our observance.

Let not feasting, football, and festivity end in forgetfulness of God.

May the desperate need of the rest of the world, and our own glorious heritage, remind us of the God who led our fathers every step of the way by which they advanced to the character of an independent nation.

May the faith and conviction of George Washington be renewed in us as we remember his words: ". . . there is no truth more thoroughly established than that there exists in the economy and course of nature an indissoluble union between virtue and happiness; between duty and advantage; between the genuine maxims of an honest and magnanimous policy and the solid rewards of public prosperity and felicity; since we ought to be no less persuaded that the propitious smiles of Heaven can never be expected on a nation that disregards the eternal rules of order and right which Heaven itself has ordained. . . ."

For if we do not have the grace to thank Thee for all that we have and enjoy, how can we have the effrontery to seek Thy further blessings? God, give us grateful hearts. For Jesus' sake. Amen.

FRIDAY, NOVEMBER 28, 1947

". . . instead of indicting other philosophies, we shall inspire our own. . . ."

Congressmen coming back from European jaunts were beginning to see the absolute necessity of exporting some of our democratic ideas and ideals along with financial aid. They were therefore ready to restore some of the 40 per cent that had been cut from appropriations for the Voice of America.

The "band wagon" was much in evidence, since the 1948 elections were in the offing.

O Lord, lift from our hearts all the discouragement, the cynicism, and the distrust of one another that destroy our faith in the little people who make up this Republic and eat at the very foundations of our democracy.

Give to our leaders faith in our way of life, so that, instead of indicting other philosophies, we shall inspire our own. Give them faith in the people, in their deep desire to do whatever is for the good of all, in their willingness to make personal sacrifices for a good cause.

May we have courageous leadership, based on faith and not on fear—leadership that goes out in front and is not forever running to catch up with a band wagon. Lord, increase our faith, through Jesus Christ our Lord. Amen.

MONDAY, DECEMBER 1, 1947

" . . . before we reach any decisions, make us willing to ask 'What would Jesus do?' . . ."

An Interim Aid Bill authorising European aid up to $397 million was proposed. Senator Vandenberg opened the debate on this with a speech which urged a bipartisan foreign policy and swift passage of the bill out of " a self interest which knows . . . we cannot indefinitely prosper in a broken world."

The Interim Aid Bill was finally passed 83-6.

As we come together in prayer, O God, we know that there is nothing in our hearts, in our minds, or in our past that we can hide from Thee, for our lives are all of one piece in Thy sight—not partitioned as we like to think.

Therefore deliver us from the error of seeking and expecting Thy guidance in our public lives while we close the door to Thee in our private living.

Help us to be good men, that we may become good leaders. For this day, before we reach any decisions, make us willing to ask, "What would Jesus do?" Then give us courage and the grace so to act. We ask it in His lovely name. Amen.

MONDAY, DECEMBER 8, 1947

Thou, O God, art our Father, and to our Father we come in this prayer. Reassure us that we have, each one, a place in Thy heart and are precious in Thy sight.

We know that we have offended Thee by some of the things we have done. We know that Thou canst not bless all that we undertake and dost not approve of all our attitudes. But we would hold on to that love Thou hast for each one of us—the love that will not let us go and will not let us off.

When we are overwhelmed by our sense of littleness in the world, may we remember that Thou hast made us all different, hast given to each of us life for a purpose, and if we fail it will never be fulfilled.

As our Lord preached some of His greatest sermons to audiences of one, may He now whisper to each one of us, as we wait upon Him, yielded and still. Amen.

WEDNESDAY, DECEMBER 10, 1947

It is good, O Lord, that it is not custom that brings us again into this sacred moment of prayer, but our deep sense of need.

Forgive us all that we talk too much and think too little. Forgive us all that we worry so often and pray so seldom. Most of all, O Lord, forgive us that, so helpless without Thee, we are yet so unwilling to seek Thy help.

Give us grace to seek Thee with the whole heart, that seeking Thee we may find Thee, and finding Thee may love Thee, and loving Thee may keep Thy commandments and do Thy will. Through Jesus Christ our Lord. Amen.

FRIDAY, DECEMBER 12, 1947

Our Father in heaven, be gracious unto Thy servants, the Senators of the United States. Give them strength for the tasks of this day and guide them in their labours.

When they are tempted to wonder if a righteous peace is not an impossible dream, remind them that Thou art not senile, or asleep, or defeated. "A different world cannot be built by indifferent people." Let us never give up hope of the possibility of change.

When we feel the pressure of crisis, remind us that Thou hast plenty of time. We have to remember that Thou art never in a hurry and wilt not be rushed by the deadlines of impatient men or by the violence of the wicked.

Give us the grace to wait upon Thee, for " they that wait upon the Lord shall renew their strength ; they shall mount up with wings as eagles; they shall run, and not be weary; and they shall walk, and not faint."

Grant these mercies unto Thy servants, through Jesus Christ our Lord. Amen.

MONDAY, DECEMBER 15, 1947

Our Father, as our heads are bowed in prayer, may our hearts be open to Thy Spirit, lest we say words with our hearts not in them and make Thee yawn at the emptiness of our petition, or make Thee angry at the insincerity of what we do.

Give us faith to believe in prayer, and in Thy willingness to work in us that Thy will may be done among the nations and in our own land. We ask this in Jesus' name. Amen.

TUESDAY, DECEMBER 16, 1947

Lord Jesus, in the hush of this moment we pray that Thy tender Spirit may steal into our hearts and reveal to us how near and how dear Thou art.

There are times when Thou art not real to us, and we know why. It is not because Thou hast withdrawn from us, but because we have wandered away from Thee; not because Thou art not speaking, but because we are not listening; not because Thy love for us has cooled, but because we have fallen in love with things instead of persons.

O Lord, melt the coldness of our hearts that we may again fall in love with Thee who didst love us. Amen.

WEDNESDAY, DECEMBER 17, 1947

Let us now rejoice, most gracious God, in the love Thou hast shown toward us, opening up to us a way whereby we might be delivered from our sin and foolishness.

We have found out that we cannot do wrong and feel right. By our tolerance of some wrongs, we have come close to being intolerant of the right.

Make us bold enough to confront the face of evil and

of wrong, even when it bears our own image. May we see that in every choice we make we are for Thee or against Thee. God, help us to keep our moral voting record straight. Through Jesus Christ our Lord. Amen.

THURSDAY, DECEMBER 18, 1947

Peter Marshall felt himself to be a possible channel of God's love and help to the Senators. The depth of his belief in prayer is clearly shown by his concern lest he be a clogged channel.

Our Father, let not my unworthiness stand between Thee and the Members of this body as we join in prayer.

Hear not the voice that speaks, but listen to the yearnings of the hearts now open before Thee in this moment when each one of us is alone with Thee.

May the love of God, which is broader than the measure of man's mind; the grace of our Lord Jesus Christ, which is sufficient for all our needs; and the fellowship of the Holy Spirit, who shall lead us into all truth, be with us all this day. Amen.

FRIDAY, DECEMBER 19, 1947

We thank Thee, O God, for the return of the wondrous spell of this Christmas season that brings its own sweet joy into our jaded and troubled hearts.

Forbid it, Lord, that we should celebrate without understanding what we celebrate, or, like our counterparts so long ago, fail to see the star or to hear the song of glorious promise.

As our hearts yield to the spirit of Christmas, may we discover that it is Thy Holy Spirit who comes—not a sentiment, but a power—to remind us of the only way by which there may be peace on the earth and goodwill among men.

May we not spend Christmas, but keep it, that we may be kept in its hope, through Him who emptied Himself in coming to us that we might be filled with peace and joy in returning to God. Amen.

The prayer which follows is probably the shortest prayer ever prayed in the Senate. Often at the close of the prayer Senator Vandenberg would whisper some comment to Peter. On this day Vandenberg smilingly commented, " Now I know just how a condemned man feels."

Our Father, who art Lord of heaven and of all the earth, Thou knowest the difficulties these men have to face and the grave decisions they must make. Have mercy upon them, for Jesus' sake. Amen.

O Saviour of the world, Thou who hast a plan for peace and a programme for all the nations, make it plain, and make us see it clearly, that we may find that which will work and will have Thy blessing.

Save us from hotheads that would lead us to act foolishly, and from cold feet that would keep us from acting at all.

May Thy Holy Spirit work among us to lead us into all truth. Through Jesus Christ our Lord. Amen.

"... Without Thee, we shall discuss more and more
    and settle less and less ..."

There was plenty for the 80th Congress to discuss and settle —the Marshall Plan for European Recovery, Universal Training, extended price supports and crop insurance, unemployment compensation, the admission to the United States of displaced persons, etc.

Lord, Thou wilt still be here after this prayer is said, and we would have it so, for we know deep down in our hearts that without Thy help we can do nothing abiding.

Without Thee we shall discuss more and more and settle less and less.

Unite, we pray Thee, the leaders of our Nation behind

the right way to achieve a just and lasting peace in our land and in all the world, that we may win it together, lest we lose it apart. Amen.

MONDAY, JANUARY 12, 1948

Lord Jesus, we need Thy power, obtained through prayer, to solve problems, and decide issues, and to do Thy will. But let us not imagine that this formal prayer can take the place of private petition. May there arise from every desk the silent prayer that seeks to know Thy will.

We long for such guidance that when a thing is right, we shall all know it; and when it is wrong, it will not be proposed. We would not run away from truth, but find a refuge in it.

We would not avoid the discipline of hard thinking, but deliver us, O Lord, from wrong thinking that leads to wrong conclusions. Guide us this day, for Thy mercy's sake. Amen.

WEDNESDAY, JANUARY 14, 1948

We are glad, our Father, that troubles are cannibals—the big ones eat up the little ones.

But it may not be so with our duties and responsibilities. Help our Senators to keep a sane perspective, lest the big issues overshadow the lesser ones, and they fail to do Thy will with them. In all things, big and little, reveal to us Thy wisdom and Thy love. Through Jesus Christ our Lord. Amen.

FRIDAY, JANUARY 16, 1948

Our Father, we turn to Thee because we are sore vexed with our own thoughts. Our minds plague us with questionings we cannot answer, and history confronts us with responsibilities we cannot evade. Who among us is sufficient for these things?

We are humbled by our experience of failure and driven by pressure to act before we are sure what Thou wouldst have us do. Thou knowest our deadlines as Thou knowest our need. We cannot push Thee, for Thou wilt not be hurried. But only Thou canst keep us from being pushed.

Give us, therefore, the unhurried mind and the untroubled heart, by the mercies of Christ our Lord. Amen.

MONDAY, JANUARY 19, 1948

O God, we turn to Thee in the faith that Thou dost understand and art very merciful.

Some of us are not sure concerning Thee; not sure how Thou dost reveal Thy will to us; not sure that it is possible for us to know, in every decision, just what Thou desirest Thy servants to do. But if we could say, " This is what God wants us to do ", none would vote against it, and how much time and temper and money would be saved.

Make each one of us willing to yield himself to Thee in prayer and obedience. Come and deliver us, O Holy Spirit, for we have no hope in ourselves. Amen.

WEDNESDAY, JANUARY 21, 1948

O Lord most high and very near, to whose mind the past and the future meet in this very day, hear us, we pray.

The great questions that stand unanswered before us defy our best wisdom. Though our ignorance is great, at least we know we do not know. When we do not know what to say, keep us quiet.

When we do not know what to do, let us ask of Thee, that we may find out. We dare to ask for light upon only one step at a time. We would rather walk with Thee than jump by ourselves. We ask this in the name of Jesus Christ, who promised to send us a guide into all truth. Amen.

MONDAY, JANUARY 26, 1948

O God, our Father, we pray that the people of America, who have made such progress in material things, may now seek to grow in spiritual understanding.

For we have improved means, but not improved ends. We

have better ways of getting there, but we have no better places to go. We can save more time, but are not making any better use of the time we save.

We need Thy help to do something about the world's true problems—the problem of lying, which is called propaganda; the problem of selfishness, which is called self-interest; the problem of greed, which is often called profit; the problem of licence, disguising itself as liberty; the problem of lust, masquerading as love; the problem of materialism, the hook which is baited with security.

Hear our prayers, O Lord, for the spiritual understanding which is better than political wisdom, that we may see our problems for what they are. This we ask in Jesus' name. Amen.

WEDNESDAY, JANUARY 28, 1948

Our Father, it seems hard to care for those we find it far easier to hate, to love those whom we regard as unlovely, to spend our lives for those who are so ungrateful.

If we are to learn, Thou must be our teacher. Since we will be criticised, let it be for doing too much or too little rather than for doing nothing.

Teach us to trust not to cleverness or learning but to that inward faith which can never be denied. Lead us out of confusion to simplicity. In the name of Jesus Christ. Amen.

FRIDAY, JANUARY 30, 1948

O Lord, our God, even at this moment as we come blundering into Thy presence in prayer, we are haunted by memories of duties unperformed, promptings disobeyed, and beckonings ignored.

Opportunities to be kind knocked on the door of our hearts and went weeping away. We are ashamed, O Lord, and tired of failure.

If Thou art drawing close to us now, come nearer still, till selfishness is burned out within us and our wills lose all their weakness in union with Thine own. Amen.

Lord, we are finding that without Thee we can do nothing. Let not foolish pride or stubborn will keep us from confessing it.

Help us, O Lord, when we want to do the right thing but know not what it is. But help us most when we know perfectly well what we ought to do and do not want to do it. Have mercy upon us, Lord, and help us for Jesus' sake. Amen.

THURSDAY, FEBRUARY 5, 1948

We confess, O Lord, that we think too much of ourselves, for ourselves, and about ourselves.

If our Lord had thought about Himself, we would not now be bowed in prayer, nor have the liberty in which and for which to pray.

If the great men whom we honour for their part in building our Nation had thought about themselves, we would have no free Republic today.

Help us to see, O Lord, that "I" is in the middle of sin, and let no man among us think more highly of himself than he ought to think, to the end that we may be used of Thee in Thy service for the good of all mankind. Through Jesus Christ our Lord. Amen.

MONDAY, FEBRUARY 9, 1948

" . . . less freedom in the world than there was before. . . ."

In January 1948 another European country—Rumania—went behind the Iron Curtain. On January 30 Gandhi had been murdered. His death dramatised the sense of frustration that pervaded the non-communist world.

Most merciful Father, strengthen our faith, we pray, and save us from discouragement. Let not our hearts fail us when, after a war to set peoples free, there is less freedom in the world than there was before.

Setting up standards of right and justice, we have seen them betrayed for money and mocked by selfishness. We have tried to forgive our enemies; we have humbled ourselves before haughty and cruel men, but we have not changed their hearts. Only Thou canst do that. But it takes faith to wait.

So we are tempted to despair of our world. Remind us, O Lord, that Thou hast been facing the same thing in all the world since time began.

But let not our hearts become hard or our spirits bitter. Keep our souls in faith and in hope. Through Jesus Christ our Lord. Amen.

WEDNESDAY, FEBRUARY 11, 1948

"... Give to the people of America, and to their leaders ... old-fashioned love of country that seeks to give rather than get. ..."

Candidates for the coming Presidential campaign seemed to be everywhere on the landscape—Harry Truman, Henry Wallace, Thomas Dewey, Stassen, MacArthur. In New Hampshire, an " Eisenhower for President " club was formed. " A Vandenberg for President " fever was growing in Michigan.

Our Father, as we remember the great men who by their trust in Thee helped to give this Nation its glorious heritage, remind us that we honour them best when we follow their good example.

Give to the people of America, and to their leaders, the old-fashioned love of country that seeks to give rather than to get. Help us to acknowledge our dependence upon the patience that forgives our failures, the truth that indicts our compromise and our hypocrisy.

We ask Thee not for tasks more suited to our strength, but for strength more suited to our tasks. May we so live that the sacrifices that have been made for our liberty shall not have been in vain. This we ask in the name of Thy dear Son, our Lord and Master, Jesus Christ. Amen.

Our Father, on this World Day of Prayer, we join the ten million women in our own country and their sisters in many other lands in this their petition for Christian fellowship and world brotherhood.

"Father of all mankind, we come in deep humility, giving Thee our thanks and praise. Here and now we confess our sins. Forgive us our mistakes and transgressions.

"Grant us faith to look with fearless eyes beyond the chaos of our world and time, knowing that out of this shall rise, lifted by Thy grace, peace with justice and a time of brotherhood.

"Vouchsafe unto us the will to work together. Create within us the unselfish purpose of Thy Son, who gave His life for all peoples, and may our deeds reflect the mind of Christ. Remove from us greed and suspicion.

"Lift us above pettiness and destroy the hate that is the great destroyer. Throughout the earth, may that which we profess come alive in human relations.

"May we serve Thee better and love Thee more, that Thy kingdom may come on earth as it is in heaven. Through Jesus Christ Thy Son, our Lord." Amen.

TUESDAY, FEBRUARY 17, 1948

Our Heavenly Father, save us from a worship of the lips while our hearts are far away.

In the battle now being fought in the realm of ideas, where deadly attacks are made upon our greatest treasure, our belief in God and the Gospel of Christ, deliver us from the peril of indifference, for we know that rust will crumble a metal when hammer blows will only harden it.

May this minute of prayer find each one of us, in his own way, reaching out for Thy help and guidance. Hear our prayers and be with us this day. We ask in Jesus' name. Amen.

O God, be merciful when we pray with half our heart or listen with half our mind, and pity us that we are torn as we are and bedevilled with compromises. Vainly we long for life without such difficult decisions, yet we know that we have only ourselves to blame for the tensions in which we live.

We need to pray that our own eyes be opened to the truth. Deliver us from the reservations that would pray: "Thy kingdom come—but not yet; Thy will be done on earth—by other people." Help each one of us to see that if Thy Holy Spirit is to lead America, He must be permitted to lead us. If Thy will is to be done, we must do it.

O God, most merciful, consider not our cowardice, but forgive our failings.

Harken to those prayers of our hearts which come to us in high moments when we forget ourselves and think of Thee. Amen.

TUESDAY, MARCH 2, 1948

O God, forgive the poverty and the pettiness of our prayers. Listen not to our words but to the yearning of our hearts. Hear beneath our petitions the crying of our need.

Thou gavest men life and at the same time gavest them liberty, and Thou must help us who love liberty to keep it in these days when it is stolen and destroyed. Help us to see that when other men lose their freedom our own freedom is threatened.

And may we meet the threats of this hour with courage and with boldness. Through Him whose truth makes us free indeed. Amen.

FRIDAY, MARCH 5, 1948

Vandenberg's European Recovery Programme was unanimously passed in the Foreign Relations Committee and sent to the floor. During the days that followed, Vandenberg bravely and effectively defended the plan on the floor of the Senate against those Senators who were not quite ready to give up their isolationism.

Peter watched, with great interest, this day-by-day sparring. He felt that the Marshall Plan was right. This is reflected in such fervent petitions as . . ." May no cowardice or callous selfishness make us reluctant to assume the responsibilities of leadership in a world hungry for hope . . ."

The European Recovery Programme finally passed the Senate 69-17.

Grant, O Lord, that this assembly of freemen, chosen to lead a nation that loves and lives its freedom, may give hope and help to all those who, loving liberty, long to live in it.

May no cowardice or callous selfishness make us reluctant to assume the responsibilities of leadership in a world hungry for hope. This we ask in the name of Jesus Christ, who is the hope of our salvation. Amen.

MONDAY, MARCH 8, 1948

Eternal God and our loving Father, we come to Thee this day in the name of Jesus Christ, who is the lover of our souls and the Saviour of all mankind.

May we feel His love and respond to it. May His Spirit shine into lives that are darkened by worry, doubt, or fear. Strengthen and guide all those who are sincerely trying to do what is right, and make it plain.

Make us more mindful of the needs of our fellow men and less absorbed in selfish concerns, that Christ may approve and bless what we do here this day. We ask these things in His name. Amen.

TUESDAY, MARCH 9, 1948

" . . . the war is not really ended. . . ."

The communist coup in Czechoslovakia had gone off as expected, and one more of freedom's lights was extinguished.

133

Another coup was expected almost daily in Finland. In Italy, communist strength was growing ominously.

Our Father, to whom all mankind is dear, if we feel frustrated in efforts to achieve a just and lasting peace, how must Thou feel that men so long and so wilfully refuse to heed Thy laws and live in Thy love.

We have found that peace does not come when the guns are silenced, for the war is not really ended. The job is not done when the fire engines drive away.

So deliver us from the blasphemy of optimism that is mere wishful thinking.

Save us from the delusion of health, that we may find the cure for our sickness. Teach us, O God, that what is needed is not new things but new spirits.

Give us the uplifted face and the flashing eye that express a purpose in life, that will make sacrifice a joy and discipline our peace. Through Jesus Christ our Lord. Amen.

WEDNESDAY, MARCH 10, 1948

O God, our Father, let us not be content to wait and see what will happen, but give us the determination to make the right things happen.

While time is running out, save us from patience which is akin to cowardice. Give us the courage to be either hot or cold, " to stand for something, lest we fall for anything." In Jesus' name. Amen.

THURSDAY, MARCH 11, 1948

" . . . May we trust, not in bombs, however powerful, but in Thee . . . in Thy plan. . . ."

Lilienthal, chairman of the Atomic Energy Commission, was pleading about this time that the temporary respite bought for us by the A-bomb must be used to spread understanding —not fear.

O Christ, who givest peace to every believing heart, bestow that gift upon us now, for we are troubled and uneasy. Events in our world take away our hope and shatter our

134

peace. We need to be reassured that peace is still possible and that God's will shall yet be done upon the earth.

We believe that God's judgments are sure and altogether right, but we do wonder how long Thou wilt suffer godless men to defy Thee and to destroy the dreams Thou hast planted in human hearts. May we trust not in bombs, however powerful, but in Thee, in Thy might, in Thy love, in Thy plan, and in our secret weapon, the prayers of them that love Thee. Through Jesus Christ our Lord. Amen.

FRIDAY, MARCH 12, 1948

Our Father, when we long for life without trials and work without difficulties, remind us that oaks grow strong in contrary winds and diamonds are made under pressure. With stout hearts may we see in every calamity an opportunity, and not give way to the pessimism that sees in every opportunity a calamity.

Knowing that Thou art still upon the throne, let us get on with the job on hand, doing the best we can and leaving the rest to Thee. Help us to show ourselves to be good workmen who need not be ashamed, rightly dividing the word of truth. This we ask in Jesus' name. Amen.

SATURDAY, MARCH 13, 1948

O Lord, direct our hearts into the patience of Christ. Make strong our faith that God's will, though it may be hindered for a time and obstructed by human blindness and folly and sin must in the end be triumphant.

May all that we do be in accordance with that victory of our God. Graciously minister to Thy servants, the Members of this body, according to their needs. Through Jesus Christ our Lord. Amen.

MONDAY, MARCH 15, 1948

O Spirit of the Living God, breathe upon this assembled company Thy gracious power. As the coming of spring rouses Nature from winter sleep, so may Thy Spirit revive us, giving us new hope and a livelier faith. If we have never before been conscious of our need, make our souls hungry for Thee, O God, that we may no longer be content to be half-alive, which is half-dead.

Give us fullness of life, set free from fear and doubt, that we may find new joy in our labours. Through Jesus Christ our Lord. Amen.

TUESDAY, MARCH 16, 1948

We pray unto Thee, O God, and call Thee our Father. Since Thou art our Father, we are Thy children; and if Thy children, we need never despair, no matter how dark and troubled our horizons.

> Teach us not to despise the life we are called to live, since it was given us by Thee.
>
> Teach us not to neglect the task of today because we cannot see its eternal effect.
>
> Teach us not to neglect the little duties which are training us for a great stewardship.

Help us to give a good account of this day for Jesus' sake. Amen.

WEDNESDAY, MARCH 17, 1948

We pray, O God, in this uncertain hour, that Thou wilt reveal Thyself and Thy will to the leaders of our Nation.

Help them to see the right way to preserve the things so dearly bought and to resolve the difficulties that seem so great.

Inspire their thoughts by the mind of Christ coming into their minds and the courage to challenge America to accept the moral responsibilities of the spiritual leadership of the world.

May we not be afraid to face facts, however unpleasant. Take away the acrophobia of our souls that we may breathe the pure air of high ideals and lofty purpose without becoming lightheaded.

For the sake of the world, for the sake of peace, for the sake of America, for conscience' sake, for God's sake, help us to do the right thing. Amen.

Our Father in Heaven, save us from the conceit which refuses to believe that God knows more about government than we do, and deliver us from the stubbornness that will not seek God's help.

Today we claim Thy promise: "If any man lack wisdom, let him ask of God, who giveth to all men liberally . . . and it shall be given him." Thou knowest, Lord, how much we need it. Make us willing to ask for it and eager to have it. In Jesus' name we pray. Amen.

O God, our Father, as a battery is recharged without sound or motion, so wilt Thou, in this moment so precious, send Thy spirit into the hearts and minds of Thy servants, the Senators of the United States.

With newness of life, with spiritual power, vision, and lively faith, enable them to meet all the demands of this day with glad anticipation, and give them peace. Through Jesus Christ our Lord. Amen.

" . . . in the midst of the dangerous opportunity that we call crisis. . . ."

President Truman called a joint session of the Congress and reported that hopes for peace were badly shaken. Jan Masaryk of Czechoslovakia had died either by suicide or by Communist hands.

Our Father, give us the faith to believe that it is possible for us to live victoriously even in the midst of dangerous opportunity that we call crisis. Help us to see that there is something better than patient endurance or keeping a stiff upper lip, and that whistling in the dark is not really bravery.

Trusting in Thee, may we have the faith that goes singing

in the rain, knowing that all things work together for good
to them that love Thee. Through Jesus Christ our Lord.
Amen.

TUESDAY, MARCH 23, 1948

This was Easter week.

Lord Jesus, in the days of this holy week of solemn remembrance, bring to our minds again Thy new commandment
that we love one another.

With loving concern in our hearts, may we cherish each
other and be willing to put the welfare of others ahead of our
own. In loving other people we shall best express our love
for Thee. So help us to love that we may be loved. For
Thy name's sake. Amen.

WEDNESDAY, MARCH 24, 1948

God of mercy and compassion, Thou knowest our nature
and readest our secret thoughts, and we can hide nothing
from Thee.

Help us, then, to lay aside every disguise we wear before
the face of man and find rest and peace in being what
we are and nothing more. Enable us to put off all sham
and pretence, so that from now on we may live a life of
freedom and sincerity.

It is not dangerous to be honest, but help each one of
us to be true to himself at his best, and make us the best
we can be, for the sake of Him who died for us all. Amen.

THURSDAY, MARCH 25, 1948

Lord Jesus, Saviour of the world, in Thy holy name we join
our hearts in prayer. This week, as we remember all Thou
didst endure for us, we may be sure Thou hast not forgotten. For we will not let Thee forget.

With every sin of ours, we renew the pain. Thy heart
did know. Every time we ignore Thee, forget Thee, and
heed not Thy way, we revive for Thee the loneliness Thou

didst feel and the spiritual blindness that broke Thy heart.

O Lord, give us Thy grace that we may not crucify Thee afresh but, loving Thee, keep Thy commandments.

With steady faith that Thy kingdom will yet be established upon the earth, help us to hasten its coming by letting Thee work in us and through us to do Thy will. Amen.

MONDAY, MARCH 29, 1948

Our hearts still singing with the beauty and joy of Easter, we pray to Thee, O Christ, to keep us under the spell of immortality.

May we never again think and act as if Thou wert dead. Let us more and more come to know Thee as a living Lord who hath promised to them that believe: "Because I live, ye shall live also."

Help us to remember that we are praying to the Conqueror of Death, that we may no longer be afraid nor be dismayed by the world's problems and threats, since Thou hast overcome the world. In Thy strong name, we ask for Thy living presence and Thy victorious power. Amen.

THURSDAY, APRIL 1, 1948

Hear, O God, our Father, the earnest supplications of the Senators gathered for this sacred moment of prayer and deepen our feelings of unity and fellowship as we pray with them and for them.

Give us wisdom to see that no good life comes without right discipline. Give us the grace to impose it upon ourselves, lest others do it for us.

Help us to discipline our speech, that we may seek clarity rather than cleverness and sincerity instead of sarcasm.

Help us to discipline our thinking and our actions, that in this place the world may see democracy at its best and us at our best for democracy and for Thee to use us. In the name of Jesus Christ, Thy Son, our Lord. Amen.

" . . . Together we pray for . . . their loved ones concerning whom they are anxious. . . ."

One of the individuals whom Peter had in mind here was Mrs Arthur Vandenberg. One day, shortly before this, Senator Vandenberg had, in conversation with Peter, revealed his deep concern for her health. Peter had replied, " Catherine and I are going to pray definitely for her." Vandenberg merely gripped Peter's hand, tears in his eyes, and turned away, unable to say anything.

Our Father, let us never be ashamed to come to Thee in prayer, for we are Thy children. Thou art our Father.

Together we pray for the Members of this body who need the healing ministry of the Great Physician and for their loved ones concerning whom they are anxious.

O Christ, our Saviour, Thou art still the sympathizing Jesus. Be near this day to those whose names we whisper in our hearts and minister to them according to their needs and Thy loving kindness.

Help those who are in trouble. Give Thy consolation to those who sorrow and Thy love to us all. In Thy name we pray. Amen.

Peter usually assiduously avoided mentioning specific political issues in his prayers. This prayer was, therefore, an exception, since it is most specific.

Italy seemed to be trembling on the brink of communism and civil war. Red boss Togliatti had bitterly denounced the Marshall Plan. The candidate for the Christian Democrats was de Gasperi.

These Italian elections were most important to the free world and to America in particular. American-Italians were urged to write relatives in Italy urging them to vote anti-communist.

The elections were decisive. Ninety per cent of Italy's voters turned out. The Christian Democrats piled up 48.7 per cent of the popular vote—Chamber of Deputies: 307

*out of 575 seats; Senate: 151 out of 350 seats. Counting
all parties, there was a landslide anti-communist vote of 18
million.*

O God, who hast made of one blood all the nations of
mankind, so that all are kinsmen, forgive the selfishness
that ignores the ties which Thou has established.

We pray today for the people of Italy that they may be
guided in the grave decisions they shortly must make. May
Thy will be done in that ancient land. Save Thy people
there from intimidation and coercion, and give them the
courage of true faith in democracy that they may be free.

May we in this free land esteem more highly our liberties,
in the light of the price others are called upon to pay. For
Jesus' sake. Amen.

WEDNESDAY, APRIL 7, 1948

O God, our Father, history and experience have given us
so many evidences of Thy guidance to nations and to individuals that we should not doubt Thy power or Thy willingness to direct us.

Give us the faith to believe that when God wants us to do
or not to do any particular thing, God finds a way of letting
us know it.

May we not make it more difficult for Thee to guide
us, but be willing to be led of Thee, that Thy will may
be done in us and through us for the good of America
and all mankind. This we ask in Jesus' name. Amen.

THURSDAY, APRIL 8, 1948

Our Father, in times of confusion, when men doubt their
beliefs and believe their doubts and are victims of ideologies
that seek to divide and conquer, give to the people of this
Nation a true appreciation of the great affirmations we hold
in common.

Let us appreciate our agreements and have the courage and
conviction to stand up for them, that we may stand united
and fearless before the world.

Direct our government that it may ever make it as hard
as possible to do wrong and as easy as possible to do right.

To that end, incline our leaders to the eternal truths Thou hast revealed in the Bible and in Thy Son, Jesus Christ, our Lord. Amen.

MONDAY, APRIL 12, 1948

Our Eternal Father, whose kindness is loving and whose patience is infinite, hear us again as we pray, not because of what we say but because of the deep need that drives us to Thee.

We rest in the thought that Thy love knows no change, else it would not love us long. We are burdened by things that do not matter, bewildered by problems of our own creation.

Thou hast made us heirs of a great heritage and trustees of priceless things, yet we forget the price that was paid for them and the eternal vigilance required to preserve them. Make us strong, O God, in conviction, with insight for our times and courage for our testing. Through Jesus Christ our Lord. Amen.

TUESDAY, APRIL 13, 1948

O Christ, our Living Lord, Thou hast brought us to this new day and further opportunity.

Help us to work with Thee that it may be a good day with good things done. We know that a " different world cannot be built by indifferent people." May there be no apathy in this place, no lukewarmness when we should be hot.

Abide with us, O Christ, that our hearts may burn within us and our imaginations be fired with Thy passion to do God's will. Amen.

WEDNESDAY, APRIL 14, 1948

Our Heavenly Father, in this moment of prayer, when there is silence in this Senate Chamber, may there not be silence in Thy presence. May our prayers be heard.

May no short circuits be made by our lack of faith,

our high professions joined to low attainments, our fine words hiding shabby thoughts, or friendly faces masking cold hearts.

Out of the same old needs, conscious of the same old faults, we pray on the same old terms for new mercies and new blessings. In the name of Jesus Christ our Lord. Amen.

THURSDAY, APRIL 15, 1948

If these moments, O Christ, can be spent in honest heart-to-heart communion with Thee, and Thou wilt give us Thy Spirit, then will our whole day be changed for us, and we shall be changed for the day. Our moods will become right, and we shall be sensitised.

Use these moments, O Lord, to make every thought and feeling what they ought to be, that we may be able to do things for Thy sake that we would not have done for our own or the sake of anyone else. Amen.

MONDAY, APRIL 26, 1948

It is not our brothers or our friends, but it is we, O Lord, who are standing in the need of prayer. Much as we would like to see this great company engaged in fervent supplication, we remember that Thou hast promised: "If any two are agreed, I will do it."

Let us not be staggered by statistics but rather by the implications of the prayers here uttered by a few. When they really move us, they can move our Nation. Let us not be the stumbling blocks. We ask in Jesus' name. Amen.

FRIDAY, APRIL 30, 1948

O God of grace and God of glory, when we resent having so many choices to make, may we remember that good character is the habit of choosing right from wrong.

Help us as a nation to see that our strongest defence lies back in home and school and church, where is built the character that gives free people the power to win their freedom and to hold it. May we never forget that it is only under God that this Nation or any nation can be free.

And when we have learned well this lesson, then shall we have for export more than money, even the faith and idealism for which all who love liberty will be willing to live. Amen.

WEDNESDAY, MAY 5, 1948

O God, our Father, come nearer to us than we have ever known and stay with us through the deliberations of this day, lest we give way to selfishness.

We pray for our country, thrust by world events into high responsibility. May she be willing to grow up and, with adult maturity, looking unto Thee for guidance and wisdom and courage, assume her role of leader among the nations.

So may her statesmen act and her people think that Thou canst bless her and use her. In Jesus' name we pray. Amen.

THURSDAY, MAY 6, 1948

" . . . to disagree without being disagreeable . . ."

At this time, there was much open disagreement between the Joint Chiefs of Staff, as well as a Navy-Air Force fight. Service rivalries were chiefly to blame.

Hear us, our Father, as we pray for a freshness of spirit to renew our faith and to brighten our hopes.

Create new warmth and love between the Members of the Senate and those who work with them, that they may go at their work not head first but heart first. May they be able to disagree without being disagreeable and to differ without being difficult.

In an atmosphere of team spirit, give them freedom to be honest without tension and frank without offence, that Thy spirit will not be driven from their midst. This we ask in Jesus' name. Amen.

Forgive us, Lord Jesus, for doing the things that make us uncomfortable and guilty when we pray.

> We say that we believe in God, and yet we doubt God's promises.

> We say that in God we trust, yet we worry and try to manage our own affairs.

> We say that we love Thee, O Lord, and yet do not obey Thee.

> We believe that Thou hast the answers to all our problems, and yet we do not consult Thee.

Forgive us, Lord, for our lack of faith and the wilful pride that ignores the way, the truth, and the life. Wilt Thou reach down and change the gears within us that we may go forward with Thee. Amen.

O God, our Father, be real to each one of us today, that we may become aware how near Thou art and how practical Thy help may be. Deliver us from going through the motions as though waiting for a catastrophe.

Save us from the inertia of futility. Revive our spirit of adventuresome faith. Give us nerve again and zest for living, with courage for the difficulties of peace. Through Jesus Christ our Lord. Amen.

Our Heavenly Father, when we have prayed for guidance and it comes, let us not think it strange if it be something we would not have thought of, for Thy thoughts are not our thoughts and our way is not Thine.

Make us eager to know Thy will and Thy way of dealing with situations, rather than devising our own plans and asking Thee to bless them.

Then shall we discover how much better is Thy way and how happy they are who walk in it. Through Jesus Christ our Lord. Amen.

O Lord our God, refresh us with Thy Spirit to quicken our thinking and make us sensitive to Thy will.

We may be unconscious of our deepest needs, accustomed to things as they are, ceasing to desire any changes. We may be unwilling to pay the price of better things.

Show us, Thy servants, the things that must be changed, that we hinder Thee no more. Amen.

The death mentioned was that of Senator John Holmes Overton of Louisiana.

Our Father in Heaven, humbly we bow in prayer this day, feeling the deep loss of our Nation and the Senate in the call that has summoned our brother into that life where "age shall not weary nor the years condemn."

Knowing in whom he placed his trust, we know that his faith was well founded.

We pray for those who loved him best and will miss him most. May they have the comforting ministry of Him who shall wipe away all tears from their eyes and is able to bind up broken hearts.

So teach us to number our days that we may apply our hearts unto wisdom.

May our sympathies be warm and real, and in our great loss may we learn better how to love one another, through Him who has promised: "Whosoever liveth and believeth in Me shall never die. Because I live, ye shall live also." Amen.

O God, at this moment the Senators and the Representatives of the people of this Nation humbly implore Thy help and guidance. Make it a sacred moment, a moment when men are aware of their need of God, a moment when answers come and guidance is given.

Often we pray for that which is already ours, neglected

and unused. Sometimes we pray for that which can never be ours, and sometimes for that which we must do for ourselves.

How many times we never pray at all, and then work ourselves to death to earn something that is ours for the asking.

Help us to understand that " faith without works is dead," and that works without faith can never live. Amen.

TUESDAY, MAY 18, 1948

O Lord, in the midst of great activity today we ask Thee to remind us often of Thine invisible presence,

 that out of confused issues may come simplicity of plan,

 out of fear may come confidence.

 out of hurry may come the willingness to wait,

 out of frustration, rest and power.

This we ask in Thine own name. Amen.

THURSDAY, MAY 20, 1948

O Lord, our God, while dealing honestly with things as they are, keep alive our hope that things may yet be better than they are.

 " Earth shall be fair and all her people one:

  Not till that hour shall God's whole will be done."

Give us faith to believe in the possibility of change, that, each in his own place, we may do all we can to change from bad to good, and from good to better, until Thou art satisfied with our labours. In the name of Jesus Christ our Lord. Amen.

MONDAY, MAY 24, 1948

Our Father in heaven, today we pray for Thy gift of contentment, that we may not waste our time desiring more, but learn to use and enjoy what we have.

We may not know everything, but we may know Thee and Thy will. We need not be rich to be generous, nor have all wisdom to be understanding. Our influence may not be great, but it can be good. Our speech may not be

eloquent, but it can be truthful and sincere. We cannot all
have good looks, but we can have good conscience, and
having that, we shall have peace of mind and need fear no
man.

May we be kind one to another, tender-hearted, forgiving
one another, even as Thou, for Christ's sake, hast forgiven
us. Amen.

TUESDAY, MAY 25, 1948

" . . . the difference between what we say and
what we do . . ."

*The prayer which follows was exceedingly plain-spoken.
The House of Representatives—in the face of previous
commitments by both chambers of Congress—lopped off
more than $2 billion from funds already authorised for the
European Recovery Programme and other foreign aid. The
point of this Congressional " economy " was apparently,
as Peter said, along the line of " winning votes in America."
This altered the European programme from one of intelligent
reconstruction to one of mere relief. Such a cut for the
Economic Co-operation Administration would brand United
States policies abroad as " capricious, unreliable, and im-
potent," and would make it harder to restore the prestige of
our Nation abroad.*

*The Senate Appropriations Committee was later to save
the day by unanimously approving restoration of all but
$245 million of ECA funds.*

Our Father, sometimes we are discouraged and disappointed
in the government of this Nation ; and the common people
of other lands, hungry for peace, cannot understand the
difference between what we say and what we do.

We have an uneasy feeling that we have not been right
or consistent and have risked the peace of the world for
lesser gains at home. Only if Thy Spirit guide our spokes-
men and shape our policies can this Nation regain the
respect of the world and merit Thy blessing. Winning peace
in the world must become more important than winning
votes in America.

God, direct our Senators to do what is right for Jesus'
sake and the sake of peace and good conscience. Amen.

O Lord, our God, have pity upon us, who have so little pity in our hearts.

We give, but not in kindness. We give because the sound of crying disturbs us, and we want to be free to look after the things that concern ourselves.

We want peace without pain and security without sacrifice. We had to accept the responsibilities of war, but we do not want to accept the responsibilities of peace.

O Lord, be patient with us.

Give us yet more time to learn what love is, and how love should act, and how love can change us as individuals and as a Nation. We pray in the name of Him who loves us all. Amen.

Lord Jesus, as Thou dost move among people and see what men are doing today, how sore must be Thy heart.

Thou whose head was cradled in straw must often reflect that straw was not as coarse as man's selfishness.

Thou whose hands were spread upon a Cross and fastened with nails must often reflect that nails were never so sharp as man's ingratitude.

Hear us as we pray for this poor blundering world, in which the nations never seem to learn how to live as brothers. They resort again and again to methods that produce only more bitter tears, methods that only add to misery and subtract nothing from problems.

Heal them that need healing, make strong the wavering, guide the perplexed, befriend the lonely, give new faith and courage to those whose spirits are low.

Lift up our heads, put a new light in our eyes and a new song in our hearts, and we will do better and be better for the sake of Thy love. Amen.

TUESDAY, JUNE 1, 1948

*On May 30, in Canada, the Fraser River had overflowed
Fraser Valley, British Columbia. Vancouver was isolated,
Air Force and civilians evacuated hundreds from the valley.
Within three days, 2,000 were forced to flee their homes.
Damage was estimated at $15 to $20 million.*

Spirit of God, come into our hearts and make us sensitive to
the sufferings of other people. We think of the victims of
flood and mishap and all those who have heavy hearts today.
May we so grow in grace that the sympathy we feel for
friends may also be felt for strangers.

    Cultivate within us

        the grace of thankful, uncomplaining hearts;

        the grace of boldness in standing for what is right;

        the grace of self-discipline;

        the grace to treat others as we would have others treat
            us;

        the grace of silence, that we may refrain from hasty
            speech;

        the grace of kindness, that wherever we go we may take
            something of the love of God.

Be with our Senators this day and bless them. We ask
in Jesus' name. Amen.

WEDNESDAY, JUNE 2, 1948

O Lord, let us never be afraid of a new idea or unreceptive
to a new thought, lest we pull down the shades of our
minds and exclude Thy holy light. When confronted by
mystery, help us to remember that we do not have to
explain all we know or understand all we believe. But give
us the grace of humility and the spirit of the open mind,
the courage to persist in face of difficulties, and a steady
confidence in the power of truth.

    Help us all to learn something this day, that we shall
be wise at its close and more ready for our eternal homes
when we are one step nearer. Through Jesus Christ our
Lord. Amen.

" . . . those in the gallery . . . the youth of America . . ."

During April, May, and June in Washington there is a constant procession of buses filled with American high-school students. Most of them visit the Senate to see it in action. Peter was aware of their fresh eagerness and impressionability.

Our Father in Heaven, as we pray for Thy blessings upon the Members of the Senate, we are not unmindful of those in the gallery who join us in this prayer.

We give Thee thanks for the youth of America, the leaders of tomorrow, the young people who shall someday take our places. We thank Thee for their faith in America and we pray that nothing done or said in this place shall cause them to think any less of the institutions we cherish.

Challenge them, we pray Thee, with the vision of good citizenship and a love for all that is good in America and a desire to make it even better, that this land that we love may become in truth and in fact God's own country. Amen.

Lord, we are ashamed that money and position speak to us more loudly than does the simple compassion of the human heart. Help us to care, as Thou dost care, for the little people who have no lobbyists, for the minority groups who sorely need justice. May it be the glory of our government that not only the strong are heard, but also the weak; not only the powerful, but the helpless; not only those with influence, but also those who have nothing but a case and an appeal.

May we put our hearts into our work, that our work may get into our hearts. Amen.

TUESDAY, JUNE 8, 1948

O Lord, our God, deliver us from the fear of what might happen and give us the grace to enjoy what now is and to keep striving after what ought to be. Through Jesus Christ our Lord. Amen.

WEDNESDAY, JUNE 9, 1948

O God, the light of those who seek Thee, grant to our minds that illumination without which we walk in darkness and know not whither we go.

Remember those who feel no need of Thee, who seem content with a careless unexamined life, whose hearts are unvisited by desires of better things. Leave them not to themselves, lest they go down to destruction.

Remember us, O Lord, who do not always remember Thee and help us to accomplish our tasks without tension or strain, that we may do good work and merit Thy blessing. For Jesus' sake. Amen.

THURSDAY, JUNE 10, 1948

". . . we are reminded how fragile is the thread of our lives . . ."

Three days earlier Representative L. Owens (Illinois) had died of a heart attack. He was only fifty.

Our Father in heaven, every day we are reminded how fragile is the thread of our lives and how suddenly we may be summoned away from the things that engross us here.

May the uncertainty of life make us the more anxious to do good while we have opportunity, for the sake of the record that has eternal implications far beyond the next election.

Since we shall be judged for every idle word, let us speak carefully, with a deep respect for the truth that cannot be twisted.

Bless each Member of this body, as Thou seest their

needs—those who are prevented by duty elsewhere from joining in this prayer, and those who appear to be so adequate for their tasks, but who need Thy help like the rest of us.

Reveal Thy love to all of us and grant us Thy peace. Through Jesus Christ our Lord. Amen.

FRIDAY, JUNE 11, 1948

Help us, our Father, to show other nations an America to imitate—not the America of loud jazz music, self-seeking indulgence, and the love of money, but the America that loves fair play, honest dealing, straight talk, real freedom, and faith in God.

Make us to see that it cannot be done as long as we are content to be coupon clippers on the original investment made by our forefathers.

Give us faith in God and love for our fellow men, that we may have something to deposit, on which the young people of today can draw interest tomorrow.

By Thy grace, let us this day increase the moral capital of this country. Amen.

SATURDAY, JUNE 12, 1948

Lord Jesus, as we pray for the Members of this body, its officers, and all those who share in its labours, we remember that Thou wert never in a hurry and never lost Thine inner peace even under pressure greater than we shall ever know.

But we are only human.

We grow tired.

We feel the strain of meeting deadlines, and we chafe under frustration.

We need poise and peace of mind, and only Thou canst supply the deepest needs of tired bodies, jaded spirits, and frayed nerves.

Give to us Thy peace and refresh us in our weariness, that this may be a good day with much done and done well, that we may say with Thy servant Paul: "I can do all things through Christ, who gives me strength." Amen.

Eternal God, who hast made us and designed us for companionship with Thee, who hast called us to walk with Thee and be not afraid, forgive us, we pray Thee, if fear, unworthy thought, or hidden sin has prompted us to hide from Thee.

Save us, we pray, from all sins of intellect, not only from the error and ignorance which belong to our frailty but from the pride that would make us think ourselves sufficient for our tasks.

Forgive us for thinking of prayer as a waste of time, and help us to see that without it our labours are a waste of effort.

O God, help us, guide us, and use us for Thy glory and our good. Through Jesus Christ our Lord. Amen.

> " . . . Thou knowest whether we have been voices or merely echoes, whether we have done Thy will or our own . . ."

The last prayer before the summer adjournment of the Eightieth Congress.

O God, our Father, in these days when men freely judge and condemn each other, remind us all of the Great Assize before which we must all someday appear.

Thou knowest whether we have been voices or merely echoes, whether we have done Thy will or our own, or worse still, have done neither.

Teach us, O Lord, that only Thy " Well done " will afford peace and everlasting happiness.

May we strive for that rather than the approval of men, which is but for a little while. In Jesus' name we pray. Amen.

O God, our Father, may the year that is past teach us and not torment. Help us to be realistic about ourselves.

May we not steal credit for success, nor deny blame for failure. Give us the grace to take things as they are, and to resolve, by Thy help, to make them what they ought to be, in the strong name of Jesus Christ our Lord. Amen.

"Our Father which art in heaven, hallowed be Thy name. Thy kingdom come. Thy will be done in earth as it is in heaven. Give us this day our daily bread. And forgive us our debts as we forgive our debtors. And lead us not into temptation, but deliver us from evil: for Thine is the kingdom, and the power, and the glory, for ever." Amen.

WEDNESDAY, JANUARY 5, 1949

Our Father in heaven, give us the long view of our work and our world.

Help us to see that it is better to fail in a cause that will ultimately succeed than to succeed in a cause that will ultimately fail.

Guide us how to work and then teach us how to wait. O Lord, we pray in the name of Jesus, who was never in a hurry. Amen.

THURSDAY, JANUARY 6, 1949

In this prayer, O God, we come to Thee as children to a loving Father. We pray that Thou wilt help our Senators to face the problems that confront them, not alone by giving them wisdom greater than their own but also by relieving their minds of all other anxieties.

May they now turn over to Thee loved ones who need the healing touch of the Great Physician, with every confidence that Thou wilt hear our prayers of intercession, and as we do the work that is before us, Thou wilt do Thy work of healing in those whom we love. May Thy help be so plain and practical in our family affairs that we shall come to believe strongly in the help Thou dost offer in our national affairs.

Deliver Thy servants from personal worries, that they may be able to give themselves wholly to the challenges of this hour. In Jesus' name we ask it. Amen.

MONDAY, JANUARY 10, 1949

Our Father, since we cannot always do what we like, grant that we may like what we must do, knowing that truth will one day be vindicated and right in the end must prevail.

Bless thy servants this day and keep them all in Thy peace. Amen.

THURSDAY, JANUARY 13, 1949

Stop us, O God, for a minute of prayer.

Stop our anxious minds from wandering, and our hearts from desiring anything but to know Thy will.

Let us stand at attention before Thee and hear what Thou hast to say to us.

We believe that Thou canst tell us not only what to do, but also how to do it.

If it needs making up our minds, Thou who didst make our minds canst show us how to make them up.

If it needs changing our minds, Thou canst work that miracle, too. Speak, O Lord, and make us hear, for Jesus' sake. Amen.

MONDAY, JANUARY 17, 1949

Help us, O God, to treat every human heart as if it were breaking, and to consider the feeling of others as we do our own.

Help us to be gentle, and to control our tempers that we may learn to love one another.

Give us the grace so to live this day, in the name of Jesus, who loves us all. Amen.

TUESDAY, JANUARY 18, 1949

Our Father in heaven, once again we offer unto Thee our grateful thanks for Thy mercy that cared for us during the night and brought us safely to this hour.

Today is the tomorrow we worried about yesterday, and we see how foolish our anxiety was.

Teach us to trust Thee more completely and to seek Thy help in all that we have to do, through Jesus Christ, our Lord. Amen.

THURSDAY, JANUARY 20, 1949

This was Inauguration Day. Peter opened the Senate with prayer, as it convened briefly, before the Senators went out to take their places on the platform in front of the Capitol close by the Presidential stand.

God of our fathers, in whom we trust, and by whose guidance and grace this Nation was born, bless the Senators of these United States at this important time in history and give them all things needful to the faithful discharge of their responsibilities.

We pray especially today for our President, and also for him who will preside over this Chamber.

Give to them good health for the physical strains of their office, good judgment for the decisions they must make, wisdom beyond their own, and clear understanding for the problems of this difficult hour.

We thank Thee for their humble reliance upon Thee. May they go often to the throne of grace, as we commend them both to Thy loving care and Thy guiding hand. Through Jesus Christ our Saviour. Amen.

MONDAY, JANUARY 24, 1949

"... Thy servant who, in his new capacity...."

Vice-President Alben W. Barkley now took Senator Arthur Vandenberg's place in presiding over the Senate.

Peter certainly had no intimation that this was to be his last prayer in the Senate. On this day, at the conclusion of the prayer, Mr John D. Rhodes walked to the elevator with him. Peter was in fine spirits and seemed to be in good health as he grasped Mr Rhodes' hand. " See you Thursday," he said.

The last paragraph of this last prayer could not more effectively summarise the ideal which Peter had consistently held up before the Senators.

Today, O Lord, as the Members of the Senate pause in this moment of prayer, we unite our petitions for Thy blessing upon Thy servant who, in his new capacity, presides over this body. We thank Thee for his long years of devoted public service, for the testimony of his life and the inspiration of his example.

May he never feel lonely in this chair, but always be aware of Thy hand upon him and Thy spirit with him.

When differences arise, as they will, may Thy servants be not disturbed at being misunderstood, but rather be disturbed at not understanding.

May Thy will be done here, and may Thy programme be carried out, above party and personality, beyond time and circumstance, for the good of America and the peace of the world. Through Jesus Christ our Lord. Amen.

THURSDAY, JANUARY 27, 1949

Early on the morning of Tuesday, the twenty-fifth, Peter awakened with severe pains in his chest and arms. It very soon became apparent that his condition was serious, and that he would have to be taken to the hospital.

One of his last requests before the ambulance came was that I ask "Cranny"—Dr Clarence Cranford, of Washington's Calvary Baptist Church—to take the Senate prayer for Thursday.

Peter died at 8.15—on the morning of the twenty-fifth. On the twenty-seventh, Dr Cranford read Dr Marshall's prayer which he had already prepared for that morning.

Deliver us, our Father, from futile hopes and from clinging to lost causes, that we may move into ever-growing calm and ever-widening horizons.

Where we cannot convince, let us be willing to persuade, for small deeds done are better than great deeds planned.

We know that we cannot do everything. But help us to do something. For Jesus' sake. Amen.

ACKNOWLEDGMENTS

Grateful acknowledgment is hereby made to the McGraw-Hill Book Company for the following prayers, which first appeared in the American edition of *A Man Called Peter*: " We Confess Before Thee," " The Cry of the Human Heart," " For More Faith "; to the *Washington Evening Star* for permission to quote three paragraphs from an article by Harold B. Rogers dated January 5, 1947; and to Mrs Daniel A. Poling and the National Council of Churches of Christ in America for permission to quote the prayer for the World Day of Prayer Service for 1948, used in the Senate prayer for February 13, 1948.

I wish to express my deep appreciation to Miss Margaret Bradley, my most efficient secretary, who typed the manuscript; to Miss Kathryn Campbell and Mr Edward MacConomy (the latter of the Legislative Reference Division of the Library of Congress) who helped with the background research work in connection with the Senate prayers; to Miss Alma Deane Fuller, Mrs George Markley, and Mrs Eugene Campagna who gave me many valuable suggestions in the final selection of the pastoral prayers; to Miss Sara Leslie who helped with the format of the book.

In public prayer one's mind instinctively recalls many passages from Scripture, hymns, and well-loved authors. I have tried to find all such quotations in the prayers and to give proper credit. If any such quotations still remain unacknowledged, the publisher or I will appreciate information to that effect and will be happy to give the usual credit in all future editions of the book.

C. M.

The quotations in the prayers on pages 94 and 106 are condensed and reprinted from *A Diary of Private Prayer* by John Baillie; by permission of the Oxford University Press.